Worm Painting

and 44 More
Hands-On Language
Arts Activities for the
Primary Grades

E. Jo Ann Belk
Mississippi State University
Meridian, Mississippi, USA

Richard A. Thompson
University of Central Florida
Orlando, Florida, USA

INTERNATIONAL
Reading
Association

800 Barksdale Road, PO Box 8139
Newark, Delaware 19714-8139, USA
www.reading.org

The International Reading Association attempts, through its publications, to provide a forum for a wide spectrum of opinions on reading. This policy permits divergent viewpoints without implying the endorsement of the Association.

Director of Publications   Joan M. Irwin
Editorial Director, Books and Special Projects   Matthew W. Baker
Special Projects Editor   Tori Mello Bachman
Permissions Editor   Janet S. Parrack
Associate Editor   Jeanine K. McGann
Production Editor   Shannon Benner
Editorial Assistant   Tyanna L. Collins
Publications Manager   Beth Doughty
Production Department Manager   Iona Sauscermen
Art Director   Boni Nash
Supervisor, Electronic Publishing   Anette Schütz-Ruff
Senior Electronic Publishing Specialist   Cheryl J. Strum
Electronic Publishing Specialist   Lynn Harrison
Proofreader   Charlene M. Nichols

Project Editors   Shannon Benner and Matthew W. Baker

Illustration   Kathleen King: cover; pp. 100, 110

Copyright 2001 by the International Reading Association, Inc.
All rights reserved. No part of this publication may be reproduced or transmitted in any form or by any means, electronic or mechanical, including photocopy, or any informational storage and retrieval system, without permission from the publisher.

Library of Congress Cataloging-in-Publication Data
Belk, Jo Ann, 1939–
    Worm painting and 44 more hands-on language arts activities for the primary grades / Jo Ann Belk, Richard Thompson.
        p.   cm.
Includes bibliographical references.
    ISBN 0-87207-290-8
    1. Language arts (Primary)   2. Education, Primary—Activity programs.   3. Effective teaching.   I. Title: Worm painting and forty-four more hands-on language arts activities for the primary grades.   II. Thompson, Richard A., 1930–.   III. Title.
    LB1528.B39   2001
        372.6—dc20   2001000534

CONTENTS

Introduction

Helping children realize their learning potential requires teachers to plan and organize their instruction and engage students in hands-on learning activities (Hardman & Mroz, 1999). Children construct their own knowledge by being actively involved in learning (May, 1998). An ancient proverb states this well: "I hear, I forget. I see, I remember. I do, I understand" (Waite-Stupiansky, 1997). The endless possibilities of student-centered activities demonstrate to teachers that instruction does not have to be dull and boring for learning to occur; when students are motivated to learn and have opportunities to participate in fun activities, learning is enhanced and students develop positive attitudes toward learning.

Worm Painting and 44 More Hands-On Language Arts Activities for the Primary Grades features unique, sometimes unconventional, hands-on activities for kindergarten through third-grade children that develop skills in the six language arts: reading, writing, listening, speaking, viewing, and visually representing. Not only do the activities emphasize these important skills, but they continue to reinforce how fun learning can be.

The activities are presented in a teacher-friendly format that is easy to follow. Each activity features the following components: Objective, Materials, Preparation, Procedure, Summary, Assessment, and Enrichment. To help you with assessment of the activities, sample checklists and rubrics are included in the appendixes, where readers also will find the IRA/NCTE Standards for the English Language Arts, Web sites for teachers and students, and publishers of student work. All the activities can be easily modified for use in any of the primary grades. One way this can be done is by simplifying the directions to the activities and using easier vocabulary words.

Nine parts are included in the book, each with five activities. Parts One through Six present activities for each of the six language arts. Part Seven includes activities that apply cooperative learning strategies through creative dramatics, Part Eight includes activities for children to apply language arts skills when using the computer, and Part Nine offers activities for using portfolios in the primary grades.

The activities included in this book will help children acquire social, emotional, physical, and cognitive skills in language arts; develop positive attitudes through successful learning experiences; and become what all teachers hope for their students: lifelong learners.

Show your students how fun learning can be!

REFERENCES

Hardman, F., & Mroz, M. (1999). Post-16 English teaching: From recitation to discussion. *Educational Review, 51*(3), 283–293.

May, F.B. (1998). *Reading as communication: To help children write and read* (5th ed.). Columbus, OH: Merrill.

Waite-Stupiansky, S. (1997). *Building understanding together: A constructivist approach to early childhood education.* New York: Delmar.

Of Teaching

BY SALLY Z. HARE

nspired by Kahlil Gibran's *The Prophet* and "Two Friends on a
Rainy September Afternoon"

"Speak to us of Teaching,"
                 they asked the Prophet.
And She spoke thusly:

What I know of Teaching
    is this:

I cannot teach anyone anything.
The way I learn best is to teach.

Teaching is a reciprocal activity with learning:
no teaching occurs if no learning occurs.

There is sometimes a differential in our perception of Time,
so that teaching and learning
appear to occur
not
in the same moment of Time.

One cannot teach without continuing to grow as a learner.

One never reaches the state of being a teacher;
One is always becoming a teacher.
One is constantly in a state of being a learner.
It is not possible to become a learner. You are.

The way I teach
    is most often
           the way I learn.

The way I learn
   is too often
            not the way
            the Hierarchy, the System, the Tradition
            teaches.

In our society, we say
Those who can, do.
Those who can't, teach.
We devalue the art of teaching
 and of learning.

We see learning
   as that which happens
            before—
   as, The child goes to school to learn.

We see teaching
   as that which happens
            to—
   as, I am teaching the child to read.

O, that we will come to value
   learning
            as the synonym of teaching,
That learning
   is the stuff of which
            Life is made.

And as Learning is
   Life,
So Teaching is Breath.

Reprinted from the *Forum*, a publication of the International Association of Invitational Education. Used with permission.

PART ONE

Improving Reading Comprehension and Word Identification Skills

To improve reading comprehension and word identification skills one must first think about how reading is defined. Ashmore (2001) defines reading as "an active, cognitive, and affective process in which the reader actively engages with the text and builds her own understanding of it" (p. 7). To develop this understanding is the primary goal of reading instruction. The means to this end is the teaching of comprehension and word identification skills to children so they will be able to understand what the author is trying to communicate. Helping children to acquire these skills should involve a balanced approach to reading instruction (Blair-Larsen & Vallance, 1999), which enables teachers to address different learning styles by combining aspects of a skills emphasis (i.e., phonics) with a meaning emphasis (i.e., whole language). Reading instruction should include a variety of activities with an assortment of materials at all levels (Ashmore, 2001).

The activities presented in Part One develop comprehension and word identification skills in primary-grade children. No reading program contains sufficient skill instruction to meet the needs of *all* students, so it is imperative that you provide additional instruction to those students who need more help in becoming fluent readers.

REFERENCES

Ashmore, R.A. (2001). *Promoting the gift of literacy: 101 lesson plans for oral and written language.* Boston: Allyn & Bacon.

Blair-Larsen, S.M., & Vallance, K.M. (1999). Comprehension instruction in a balanced reading classroom. In S.M. Blair-Larsen & K.A. Williams (Eds.), *The balanced reading program: Helping all students achieve success* (pp. 37–52). Newark, DE: International Reading Association.

Objective

The students will be able to answer comprehension questions after reading a story.

MATERIALS

- poster board
- dial
- pointer
- markers

PREPARATION

Cut a round circle from the poster board and with a marker divide the circle into eight pie-shaped parts. Color each part a different color. Attach a pointer to the center of the circle. Write questions or instructions concerning a story on each of the eight parts of the circle. Use general questions that would fit any story. For example, Where did the story take place? Who are the main characters? What was the most exciting part of the story?

PROCEDURE

Ask the children to read a story silently. Next, tell them there will be a game, and explain that this game will be used in the future so they should always read carefully. Divide the class into two teams and spin the dial; where the pointer lands will be the question the first team must answer. If the team answers correctly they receive one point; if the team answers incorrectly, give the question to the next team. If the second team answers the question correctly, then they also should be asked the next question. Score two points if they answer the other team's question correctly and one point if they answer their own question correctly. If the second team can answer only their question, then again score for them only one point and give the unanswered question to the opposite team and so on. After all questions on the game board have been answered correctly, the team with the highest score wins. The points are then converted to play money and thus the team becomes "millionaires." At the end of the game the play money can be used by the winning team to purchase prizes such as stickers or a homework pass.

SUMMARY

This activity motivates children to think about what they are reading and to recall information. Using play money is a good way to integrate math skills into this activity. Any story can be used with this activity.

ASSESSMENT

Observe children's ability to recall information by using a rubric to determine the accuracy, significance, and details of the information recalled (see Appendix A for a sample rubric).

ENRICHMENT

The activity may be made more challenging by changing the questions to more open-ended ones that help children to develop creativity and critical thinking skills. For example, What do you think would happen if...? or What would be a different solution the main character could have used to solve the problem? If this procedure is used the teacher or the class would determine the feasibility of the answers to decide if points would be given.

Objective

The students will develop comprehension skills through the use of synonyms.

MATERIALS
• sets of red and blue 3"✕5" index cards
• list of definitions
• red and blue construction paper

PREPARATION
Cut out two construction paper flower centers (circles) and two sets of 10 petals. Make one of the centers and petal sets blue and the other red. Construct a list of definitions. For each definition there must be two words that fit the definition (synonyms): Write one on a blue card and the other on a red card.

PROCEDURE
Give each student one card. Those students with red cards belong to the red flower team, and those students with blue cards belong to the blue flower team. The teacher or leader reads one definition for which there are two answers, or synonyms. For example, read a definition such as "a sweet liquid made by boiling sugar with water." One student might hold up the red card that reads *molasses,* and the other student with the blue card might hold up the synonym card that reads *syrup.* The first student to hold up the card with the correct synonym wins a point for his or her team. Points are shown by adding a petal to the team's flower, which can be taped to the chalkboard. The first team to complete its flower with all 10 petals attached wins the game.

SUMMARY

This activity helps to develop general comprehension skills. Synonyms can be selected from a reading list or spelling list.

ASSESSMENT

Observe the number of words children can define and pronounce. If children miss several words or definitions from the vocabulary list, provide additional practice. This practice also can be provided by a peer tutor.

ENRICHMENT

Children can construct crossword puzzles using the words and definitions. They can exchange puzzles with a partner and each person can solve the puzzle.

Objective

The students will identify different words by combining consonant digraphs or clusters with vowel phonograms.

MATERIALS

- ball pattern (circle about 1 inch in diameter cut from construction paper)
- bat pattern (rectangle about 3 inches long and 1 inch wide cut from construction paper)
- scissors
- markers

PREPARATION

Construct 20 balls using the ball pattern (circle). On each ball write one of the following consonant digraphs or clusters: *ch, sh, th, wh, ph, thr, shr, br, cr, dr, fr, gr, pr, tr, bl, cl, fl, gl, pl,* or *sl.* Construct 10 baseball bats (rectangle shape) using the bat pattern. On each bat, write one of the following sets of vowel phonograms: *ack, ail, ain, ake; ame, an, ank, ap; ask, at, ate, ay; eat, ell, est, ice; ick, ide, ight, ill; in, ine, ing, ink; ip, ock, op, uck; ig, unk, ale, aw; ir, oke, ore, ump; or, ang, oast, oom.* Next create a baseball field in the classroom by designating one corner of the room for each base, including home plate.

PROCEDURE

Divide the class into two teams and decide on a name for each team. One player from the first team selects a bat. Explain to the children that in a real baseball game the pitcher throws a ball to the hitter; however, in this game the pitcher hands the paper ball to the hitter. The player then forms a word using the beginning sound spelling on the ball and one or more of the vowel spellings on the bat. If the player can use all four vowel spellings to make a word, he or she earns a home run. A triple is earned for three, a double for two, and a single for one. If the player is unable to form a word, an out is earned. Each player moves the number of bases earned and the game continues. After three outs, the second team bats. After a designated time period the team with the most runs wins the game.

SUMMARY

This provides an excellent way to help children recognize words by analyzing the different parts of the words and blending the sounds.

ASSESSMENT

Use a checklist to record which consonant digraphs or clusters and phonograms the children have trouble blending during the game. Note these consonant digraphs or clusters and phonograms and provide additional practice for the children in blending these particular ones. This could be done in a learning center or in small groups using this game or a similar game.

ENRICHMENT

For children who make home runs, a challenge match may be played using bats with more difficult phonograms.

Word Relay

Objective

*Students will increase their sight-word vocabularies
by playing a relay game using sight words.*

MATERIALS
• index cards

PREPARATION
Print sight words on index cards and divide the class into teams.

PROCEDURE
Ask the teams to form two lines, then show the children at the front
of the lines a word card taken from the sight-word list. The first
child who pronounces the word keeps the card for his or her
team. (It is a good idea to have two copies of the word in case
both teams pronounce the word at the same time.) As soon as a
student reads a word, he or she moves to the back of the line. The
student who does not pronounce the word stays at the front of his
or her line and tries again with the next word. After all words
have been called, the teams count the number of cards they have.
The team with the most cards is the winner.

SUMMARY
This activity helps to increase children's sight vocabulary, which in
turn increases reading fluency in all subject areas.

ASSESSMENT
Use a checklist to record children's knowledge of sight words.

ENRICHMENT
Children can create crossword puzzles or stories using a list of
sight words.

Shoebox Shuffle

Objective

The students will be able to match vocabulary words with their definitions.

MATERIALS

- index cards
- four shoeboxes

PREPARATION

Draw a racetrack on the chalkboard and divide the class into two teams. Using a list of vocabulary words and matching definitions, write each vocabulary word on two index cards (one for each team). Place the four shoeboxes on the floor to designate a starting line, and choose a finishing line such as your desk.

PROCEDURE

Give each student a vocabulary card. (The words on the cards are the same for both teams.) Define a word, and two team players who have the word that fits the definition should race to the starting line and each step into two shoeboxes. With the shoeboxes on their feet, the children shuffle or slide on the carpet to the finish line and say the word. The player who gets to the finish line first scores a point for his or her team.

SUMMARY

This activity motivates students to increase their vocabulary. For young children, sliding in the shoeboxes helps develop motor skills.

ASSESSMENT

Use a checklist to note the number of words students can define.

ENRICHMENT

Students may use the words to construct stories.

PART TWO

Developing Writing Skills

Writing as a way of conveying thoughts is recognized as being a very important skill (Tiedt, Tiedt, & Tiedt, 2001), and it is necessary for social, personal, and professional purposes throughout one's life (Rubin, 2000). Children should acquire writing skills at an early age. They should write every day using a variety of types of writing (Pappas, Kiefer, & Levstik, 1999), including stories, reports, poems, and journals. This writing may be on teacher-assigned topics or topics the children choose. The classroom environment for writing should be one that promotes ownership, freedom, risk-taking, and appropriate instruction when needed (Solley, 2000).

The teacher and the child can select samples from different types of writing the child has done to be placed in a literacy portfolio, a collection of the child's writing samples. Each sample should be dated. Keeping writing samples of the child's writing over a period of time provides the teacher with an excellent way to assess writing progress. This portfolio will help you to determine strengths and weaknesses the child needs to address in his or her writing.

The writing workshop is an effective way to teach writing in the primary grades (Muschla, 1993). There are different variations of the writing workshop model, although most models contain the following format:

1. Five- to ten-minute minilesson focusing on a skill or concept.
2. Student writing for 20–25 minutes with teacher guidance. (The student writing may be journal writing, stories, poems, or other types of writing.)
3. The last 10–15 minutes of the class are used to share the writings.

The children may share their writings in different ways such as an author's chair. A desk or chair is placed at the front of the classroom where the child reads his or her writing to the class. Peers may ask questions or make suggestions. Children may share their writing in small groups or pairs.

Solley (2000) describes 25 years of research concerning the best way to teach writing. The questions addressed in the research were, Should writing be taught as a process with the tools of writing taught within context? Or should the tools of writing (grammar, parts of speech, mechanics, and spelling) be taught first and writing instruction later? She concludes that research supports teaching writing as a process approach. Whichever strategy you choose to teach writing, developing children's written expression skills is a difficult task. It demands much imagination on the part of the teacher, and requires the goals of improving technical skills such as sentence sequence and paragraphing and stimulating creative writing abilities. The activities in this part are designed to help you accomplish these goals.

REFERENCES

Muschla, G.R. (1993). *The writing workshop survival kit.* New York: The Center for Applied Research in Education.

Pappas, C.C., Kiefer, B.Z., & Levstik, L.S. (1999). *An integrated language perspective in the elementary school: An action approach* (3rd ed.). Reading, MA: Addison-Wesley.

Rubin, D. (2000). *Teaching elementary language arts: A balanced approach* (6th ed.). Boston: Allyn & Bacon.

Solley, B.A. (Ed.). (2000). *Writers' workshop: Reflections of elementary and middle school teachers.* Boston: Allyn & Bacon.

Tiedt, P.L., Tiedt, I.M., & Tiedt, S.W. (2001). *Language arts activities for the classroom* (3rd ed.). Boston: Allyn & Bacon.

Introduce Yourself

Objective

The students will introduce themselves to their classmates through descriptive writing.

MATERIALS

- writing materials including crayons
- the book *Sarah, Plain and Tall* by Patricia MacLachlan

PREPARATION

Discuss with the class the importance of knowing their classmates and the idea of the classroom as a community. In this community everyone cooperates and works together to make the classroom an inviting place to learn. In order to accomplish this, classmates must be able to get acquainted with one another.

PROCEDURE

Read *Sarah, Plain and Tall*. Tell the children that in order for Sarah to be recognized when she arrived at the train station, she had to describe herself in her letters. Her description needed to be so accurate that whoever met her at the station would recognize her. Tell the children that in order to get to know their classmates they must be able to recognize one another. Students should write a description of themselves. This should include the way they look (eye color, hair, height, etc.), three things they enjoy doing, and three things they dislike. Students also should describe something unique about themselves (for example, they have visited a foreign country or have a special hobby), and describe something that made them extremely happy. Students should not put their name on the paper.

Ask the children to exchange papers with two or three classmates so the child who gets the paper doesn't know the author. Ask each student to read the paper that he or she has, and the other children should try to guess the person who is described.

SUMMARY

This is a good activity to use at the beginning of the year to help the children get acquainted with each other.

ASSESSMENT

Observe children's ability to write a descriptive paragraph. Use a rubric for writing paragraphs (see Appendix A).

ENRICHMENT

Write a description of a character in a book read by the class. Ask the class to guess the character and the book he or she appears in.

Wishing on a Star

Objective

The students will be able to express themselves through creative writing.

MATERIALS

- stories or poems on wishing such as *The Fairies* by Rose Fyleman and the Mother Goose poem "Star Light, Star Bright"
- writing materials
- crayons or paints
- paper with a large star drawn on it and blank lines for creative writing

PREPARATION

Direct a discussion with the class on wishing and ways of wishing. Ask the class to answer the question, What is one wish you hope to achieve before you die? Answers might be "fly a plane," "go to college," "become an artist," etc.

PROCEDURE

Ask the children if they know any poems on wishing; if so, they should be encouraged to share them with the class. Then read *The Fairies* and "Star Light, Star Bright." Ask several children what they would wish for if they had a wish that would come true. Give each child the sheet of paper with the star that has blank lines for writing, and instruct each child to write a creative expression about something he or she is "wishing on a star." Color and cut out the star. Use the stars to construct a "wishing star bulletin board" or make a mobile by hanging the stars from the ceiling using paper clips and coat hangers.

ASSESSMENT

Observe participation and creativity in the writing. A checklist or rubric may be used (see Appendix A for examples).

ENRICHMENT

Create a book by compiling the star papers, adding a cover, and stapling them together. Let the children work in small groups to extend the writing to describe what might happen if one of their wishes actually came true.

Treasure Hunt

Objective

The students will be able to write clear, concise directions after playing the treasure hunt game.

MATERIALS
• envelopes
• treasure box with prize inside

PREPARATION
Divide the class into six groups of four children each. Hide the treasure box (in the library, principal's office, on the playground, etc.).

PROCEDURE
Five of the groups will write directions to different points along the path to the hidden treasure, and the sixth group will follow those directions to find the treasure. For example, group one may write the following directions:

1. Turn left at the door.
2. Follow the walk past three trees.
3. Take four giant steps north.

At this point in the hunt an envelope should be placed with directions from group two. Group two should write directions from this point to a particular place where there will be directions from group three, etc. The envelope from group five will contain the final directions indicating where the treasure can be found. When the sixth group locates the treasure (stickers, candy, etc.), all groups will share it.

SUMMARY

This activity helps children understand the importance of writing clear directions and following directions.

ASSESSMENT

Use a checklist to evaluate social skills related to group work (see Appendix A). Check written directions for clarity and grammar. For example, did the group write complete sentences? Is the punctuation correct?

ENRICHMENT

Ask children to write directions to their homes and draw maps showing how to get there in case of an emergency.

Five-Alive

Objective

*The students will develop observational skills
to aid writing.*

MATERIALS

• blank journals for student writing

PREPARATION

Explain to the children that you are going to provide them with an
experience that will help them with their writing. Tell them they will
go outside the classroom to observe an object or event. As they
observe the object or event, they are to use as many of their five
senses as they can such as hearing, smelling, seeing, or touching.
Tell them they are to look for details and relationships in the things
they observe. Explain to them that this will help them in their
writing by providing an outline. The topic will be the object or
event they are observing; the relationships will be details to add
to the topic. For example, if they are observing the playground
(topic) they may notice the equipment on the playground such as
swings (details). The swings may attract children who are playing
on the playground (details).

PROCEDURE

Take the class outside to the playground or on a nature walk if the
school has one. Ask the children to choose a spot to observe. They
should stay in that spot and observe for 10–15 minutes, then
record in their journals the things they observe and their
relationship. Give the children the following suggestions to guide
their observations: Describe the place you chose to observe. What
do you see? What do you smell? What do you hear? What can
you touch? How does it feel? What relationships do you observe
(squirrels in trees, insects, etc.)?

SUMMARY

This activity is a good way to integrate science and social studies skills into a writing activity. This writing activity is highly motivational to children because it gives them an opportunity to use a learning environment outside the classroom. Sometimes the most difficult part of writing is thinking of a topic, but this activity gives the children a topic and details to include about the topic.

ASSESSMENT

Check the children's writing by using a rubric (see Appendix A).

ENRICHMENT

Have the children work in groups to discuss an environmental problem they observed in the school (for example, littering). Have them write a letter to the principal explaining the problem and suggesting possible solutions to the problem (for example, a particular grade may be responsible for keeping a certain area of the playground litter free).

Objective

The students will be able to write a paragraph using the correct format after teacher demonstrations and completing the writing activity.

MATERIALS

- boxes of various sizes and shapes
- writing materials

PREPARATION

Collect boxes of different sizes and shapes. Give the boxes intriguing labels to spark the students' curiosity:

> *Captain Blue Beard's Treasure Chest*
>
> *Nurses' and Doctors' Kits*
>
> *Space Parts*
>
> *Danger! Do Not Open*

Place the boxes on a table in the front of the classroom.

PROCEDURE

Say, "Class, I have some boxes here that are mysterious and magical at the same time. For instance, look at this box. What do you think is inside it? Where did it come from? Who did it belong to? Use your imagination and write a paragraph about one of these boxes." Write a sample paragraph on the board with assistance from the students.

SUMMARY

This activity sparks children's curiosity and encourages creative writing.

ASSESSMENT

Check the paragraph form using a rubric (see Appendix A).

ENRICHMENT

Ask the children to work individually or in small groups to create a story about one of the boxes. The story should have at least three paragraphs.

PART THREE

Building Oral Communication Skills

Oral communication skills are the foundation on which all language skills are built. Whether the skills are receptive or expressive, speaking and listening are of prime importance, and children's acquisition of these skills bears directly on their reading and writing skills. Children learn language informally through use. They learn language as a whole rather than in discrete parts, they are creative with language, and they create new words to convey meaning. When children enter school at age 5 or 6, they have mastered most of the basic forms of their language and have developed an extensive vocabulary (Brewer, 2001). Although children have mastered these basic language forms, further development and refinement of these skills should be a major part of the language arts program in the primary grades.

In building language skills, teachers need to talk with the children and listen attentively, and they should provide children with opportunities to talk with the teacher and other classmates. May (1998) describes the importance of communicating as a way of demonstrating higher level thinking skills. He based this on Vygotsky's (1934/1986) theory that children's thinking abilities develop as a result of communicating with others. Opportunities to communicate with others may be provided by using literature, which will help develop children's oral language skills. The language children hear in books is incorporated into their own speech, and their vocabulary increases. The teacher should read to his or her class daily, and children should be encouraged to read on their own as well.

Storytelling is another way of developing oral language because children are practicing using language as they tell stories and they are hearing language spoken as they listen attentively to the stories being told. Other ways to help develop oral language include chants, finger plays, and reciting poetry. Listening to music, singing, and participating in drama and puppetry also help develop oral language.

Children learn language by using language. They need the opportunity to work together in cooperative learning groups to engage in conversations. They need to be able to talk to others and listen to others to develop their language skills (Essa, 1992). Norton (1993) describes a classroom environment that promotes oral language development as one that includes ample opportunity for children to practice oral communication. Tiedt, Tiedt, and Tiedt (2001) explain,

> An effective language arts teacher will create a classroom environment that is teeming with opportunities for exploratory talk, as students talk out loud and listen to each other in order to learn about themselves and about the world. When students work in groups and engage in collaborative talk, or use language to communicate with real people in real situations (e.g., interviews), they are building the foundation for all later learning. (p. 13)

Using oral language effectively in communicating with others will determine to a large extent the success or failure of children now and in the future. The following activities are designed to provide children with opportunities to develop effective oral language skills.

REFERENCES

Brewer, J.A. (2001). *Introduction to early childhood education: Preschool through primary grades* (4th ed.). Boston: Allyn & Bacon.

Essa, E. (1992). *Introduction to early childhood education.* New York: Delmar.

May, F.B. (1998). *Reading as communication: To help children read and write* (5th ed.). Columbus, OH: Prentice Hall.

Norton, D.E. (1993). *The effective teaching of language arts* (4th ed.). New York: Macmillan.

Pappas, C.C., Kiefer, B.Z., & Levstik, L.S. (1999). *An integrated language perspective in the elementary school: An action approach* (3rd ed.). Reading, MA: Addison-Wesley.

Rubin, D. (2000). *Teaching elementary language arts: A balanced approach* (6th ed.). Boston: Allyn & Bacon.

Tiedt, P.L., Tiedt, I.M., & Tiedt, S.W. (2001). *Language arts activities for the classroom* (3rd ed.). Boston: Allyn & Bacon.

Vygotsky, L.S. (1986). *Thought and language* (A. Kozalin, Trans.). Cambridge, MA: MIT Press. (Original work published 1934)

Family Facts

Objective

The students will improve communication skills through speaking and listening activities.

MATERIALS

- tape recorder
- writing materials

PREPARATION

Explain to the students the importance of oral history. Discuss how the world was different in the days of their grandparents or great-grandparents. Talk about the importance of the family and knowing about family history.

PROCEDURE

Ask the children to interview their grandparents or great-grandparents in person or over the telephone about the ways the world has changed since they were young. If the child's grandparents are no longer living, suggest that the child interview another relative or a family friend who is older than his or her parents. At the beginning of the interview, the children are to introduce the people they are interviewing. The time and date should be included as well as the setting. Give the children sample interview questions to ask such as, What were cars and airplanes like? What did children do for fun? How were clothes different? What was different about the schools? The children should record the interviews on paper or they may use a tape recorder. Allow the children several days to complete the interviews, then they can share their information with the class.

SUMMARY

This activity provides children with an opportunity to learn about their extended families. They should keep the interviews for future generations to share information about their families.

ASSESSMENT

Use a checklist to record your observations of the children's oral communication skills. Tape record the interviews as they are shared in class. Let each child listen to his or her interview and do a self-evaluation of oral language skills.

ENRICHMENT

Divide the class into small groups. Place those children who have similar stories in the same group, where they can use the information collected from the interviews to write a local history. Compile the different groups' stories together to form a book about the local history.

Choral Reading

Objective

*The children will develop interpretive skills
and speak in clear, rhythmic voices.*

MATERIALS

- book of poems that have familiar words and easily
  recognizable rhythms such as Robert Louis Stevenson's
  "From a Railway Carriage"

PREPARATION

Read the poem to familiarize the class with the theme, then ask
the students to read the poem orally.

PROCEDURE

Select a poem with dialogue and divide as follows: Children with
deeper voices may portray big, gruff characters such as giants,
monsters, or large animals. Children with medium voices can
speak the descriptive, narrative parts. Children with soft voices
may speak as fairies, butterflies, or small animals. For example,
"The Owl and the Pussycat" is a good poem for dialogue content.
The owl's lines would be read by the boys, and the pussycat's by
the girls. Let the children practice saying the poem using the
different voices. Tape record the poem as the children read it,
then listen to the tape and note the rhythm heard in the poem.

SUMMARY

This is a good way to motivate students to enjoy poetry. Choral
reading of poetry helps develop reading, listening, and speaking
skills, and it is especially good for children who speak English as
a second language.

ASSESSMENT

Observe children's ability to pronounce words clearly and distinctly. Ask them to interpret the meaning of the poem to assess their comprehension.

ENRICHMENT

Children may work in small groups and select a poem to read chorally, or they may create their own poems to do choral readings. They can read the poems to the class and compile the poems in a book.

Puppet Show

Objective

The students will develop positive self-concepts and communication skills through the use of puppets.

MATERIALS

- Styrofoam balls (different sizes)
- yarn (for hair)
- felt
- scraps of cloth materials (for costumes)
- construction paper
- paints
- paper sacks
- cardboard box (for stage)
- cloth (for curtain)
- tape recorder and soft music tape

PREPARATION

Tell children that they are going to do a fun activity. Give them supplies to make puppets, and allow the children to be creative and construct their own puppets. The puppets don't have to be alike; each can be different. Students will then use their puppets to dramatize situations you give to them or a story they have read.

PROCEDURE

Explain how puppets are constructed. Show children a model of one that you have constructed, but explain that their puppets do not have to look like the model. Tell them to be creative in designing their puppets. Explain the purpose of the tape recorder (to set the mood or provide background music). Divide the class into groups and let each group select a situation to dramatize or a story to portray. The students introduce the characters, then begin the puppet show.

SUMMARY

You can create situations such as, "You found five dollars on the school playground today. What should you do?" "Another child told you he brought a gun to school today. What would you do?" By having the children respond to situations such as these, character education can be integrated into the curriculum.

ASSESSMENT

Observe communication skills and group participation skills, and use a checklist to record these observations (see Appendix A).

ENRICHMENT

Children can work together in pairs or small groups to write their moral dilemma to act out in a puppet show.

Tag-Team Storytelling

Objective

The students will develop creativity and critical thinking skills by using pictures to compose a story.

MATERIALS

• folders
• a variety of pictures
• tape recorder

PREPARATION

Place one picture in each folder and give each child a folder. Tell the children in advance not to open the folders until called on.

PROCEDURE

Start telling a story, then point to a child with a folder. The child should look at the picture and continue telling the story, with his or her part of the story related to the picture in the folder. The rest of the students do the same as it comes their turn. The last child ends the story. Tape the activity and play it back for the children to listen to.

SUMMARY

This is a good activity to encourage creativity and critical thinking skills. As the children use their pictures to add to the story they must decide how the pictures relate to the story. This requires them to analyze the story and decide how the picture will fit.

ASSESSMENT

Observe the children's correct use of language and design a rubric to assess their additions to the story (see Appendix A for a sample rubric). Elements such as creativity, feasibility, originality, and interest may be included in the rubric.

ENRICHMENT

Children may use discarded magazines to cut pictures from and design their own folders to be used in telling stories. This may be done in small groups or in learning centers.

Objective

The students will improve their oral communication skills through retelling stories using a psychomotor activity.

MATERIALS
- narrative story such as a tale tall
- volleyball

PREPARATION

Explain to the class that you are going to read them a story. Instruct them to listen carefully in order to answer questions about the story. Tell them that as they answer the questions, they must use whole sentences and speak correctly.

PROCEDURE

Read the story to the class. Tell the students they are going to play a game to help them practice oral communication skills. Tell them that they are to be able to answer questions you ask them about the story. They must use complete sentences and speak correctly as they answer the questions. If they do not, another student will be chosen to answer the question. Explain that a student will pitch a volleyball to someone after you ask a question about the story. The student who catches the ball must answer the question using a correctly spoken complete sentence. If the student can't answer the question, he or she is to say "ball" and pitch the ball back to the same student. If the student answers the question correctly, he or she gets to pitch the ball to another student when the teacher asks another question about the story. The class should continue pitching the ball until all the students have had a chance to catch the ball and answer a question. You should ask different types of questions about the story, for example, What do you think would have been a better solution to the problem the main character faced? What was the most exciting part of the story?

SUMMARY

This is a good way to emphasize the importance of speaking correctly and using complete sentences when responding to questions. The game helps the students to realize the importance of using good oral communication skills. Pitching the ball is a good way to include motor skills and involve students in physical activity.

ASSESSMENT

As the students answer questions about the story, note whether or not they speak correctly using complete sentences and pronounce words correctly. Pronounce the words correctly for students who mispronounce them, and correct the use of slang words and incomplete sentences. For a written assessment, construct a list of incomplete sentences and ask students to change the incomplete sentences into complete sentences.

ENRICHMENT

Children can use index cards to write questions about the story. They should write answers on the back of the cards, then work in pairs and exchange cards to answer the questions.

PART FOUR

Developing Listening Skills

ecause listening is the first language art that children acquire, this skill is extremely important. As Rubin (2000) notes, "The child's initial learning of language comes through listening; it is the foundation for the sequential development of language arts" (p. 62). Farris (1993) also points out, "Amazingly within two weeks after birth, a baby can distinguish its mother's voice from the voices of other adults" (p. 25). Children spend most of the school day listening, because it is their primary mode of learning. They listen to learn language, follow directions, learn new concepts, participate in discussions, and engage in conversations and numerous other activities throughout the day.

Listening skills are critical in developing speaking, reading, and writing, which are all aspects of language development (Yopp & Yopp, 2001). Norton (1993) reviewed research concerning developing listening skills and offered the following recommendations for developing these skills:

Give students a specific purpose for listening because they listen differently for different purposes.

Provide a classroom atmosphere that is conducive to listening.

Provide opportunities for students to apply listening skills in new situations.

Use methods of teaching that help students acquire effective listening skills.

Some example listening activities may include listening to follow directions, listening to a story to answer comprehension questions, listening to music to identify different musical instruments, and identifying different sounds from a recording (such as farm animals).

Listening skills are critical in the development of all the language arts. Because listening is the foundation for the language arts, teachers must help children to become effective listeners. The following activities provide a number of ways that teachers can do this.

REFERENCES

Farris, P.J. (1993). *Language arts: A process approach.* Madison, WI: Brown & Benchmark.

Norton, D.E. (1993). *The effective teaching of language arts* (4th ed.). New York: Macmillan.

Rubin, D. (2000). *Teaching elementary language arts: A balanced approach* (6th ed.). Boston: Allyn & Bacon.

Yopp, R.H., & Yopp, H.K. (2001). *Literature-based reading activities* (3rd ed.). Boston: Allyn & Bacon.

Acting Out

Objective

The students will develop listening skills and be able to follow a sequence of directions by using actions to illustrate sequence.

MATERIALS

• narrative story about animals

PREPARATION

Read an animal story such as the *The Velveteen Rabbit* by Margery Williams or *The Tale of Peter Rabbit* by Beatrix Potter to the children. The following excerpt is an example: "Peter wiggled under the fence. Suddenly he stopped stock-still and listened. Then he sniffed the air. Next he gave a frightened moan and hid in the wood shed."

PROCEDURE

The children will dramatize the action suggested by the story. Tell the children that you're going to read them a paragraph from the story, and instruct them to listen carefully. When you have finished reading, choose someone to pretend to be the animal and act out what you read in the exact order that you read it. Begin with one or two sentences and increase the number as the children's listening efficiency increases.

SUMMARY

This activity will enable children to improve their listening skills and help them to become aware of the importance of sequence in following directions.

ASSESSMENT

Use a checklist to assess children's listening skills by observing how well they demonstrate the sequence of the actions (see Appendix A).

ENRICHMENT

Children may create their own stories and role-play the stories in small groups. They may then do the role-play for the other classes.

Objective

The students will develop listening and psychomotor skills through the use of finger plays.

MATERIALS

- finger plays or poems that the class can say and use actions with

PREPARATION

Tell the students that you are going to say a poem and add actions. Read the poem and do the actions two or three times until the children become familiar with the poem and actions. Tell the children that they should listen and then repeat the poem and perform the accompanying actions together.

PROCEDURE

Tell the children to repeat the poem and do the actions together in unison. A good poem that children really enjoy is "Five Little Monkeys." Read the poem aloud and incorporate actions as follows:

> Five little monkeys swinging on a tree (hold hands down and swing side to side). Teasing Mr. Alligator, "You can't catch me!" (put thumbs on ears and wiggle fingers). Along came Mr. Alligator as quiet as could be (clasp hands together) and snapped that monkey right out of that tree (snap fingers)!

Repeat using four little monkeys, three little monkeys, two little monkeys, and one little monkey.

SUMMARY

Finger plays are fun ways to help children develop listening skills. The children must listen carefully for directions to be able to do the actions and they must listen attentively to be able to repeat the finger plays. The children also develop fine motor skills as they do actions with their hands and fingers.

ASSESSMENT

Assess the development of psychomotor skills by observing children's actions. A checklist can be used to determine listening skills (see Appendix A).

ENRICHMENT

Children can work in small groups to write their own finger plays and create appropriate actions. These can then be performed for the class.

Popsicle Props

Objective

*The students will develop listening skills
by listening to a story.*

MATERIALS

- narrative stories such as *The Brave Little Tailor* by the Brothers Grimm
- popsicle sticks
- drawings of an overcoat, jacket, vest, cap, and button

PREPARATION

Draw, color, and cut out pictures of an overcoat, jacket, vest, cap, and button. Glue each item to a separate popsicle stick to make puppets. Tell the children that they are to listen to the story very carefully because you will ask them questions about the story.

PROCEDURE

Read the following story to the class using the drawings glued on the popsicle sticks as props:

> Once upon a time there was a very poor tailor. He always wanted beautiful clothes but never had the money to buy them. One day he made a suit for someone and had enough of the material left over for a beautiful overcoat (hold up the popsicle stick with the overcoat glued to it). He made the overcoat and he was so proud of the overcoat. It was so beautiful! He thought he looked so handsome while wearing it. He wore it everyday. He wore it and wore it until it was all worn out...except for enough material to make a fine jacket (hold up the popsicle stick with the jacket glued on it). It was so beautiful! He thought he looked so handsome while wearing it. He wore it everyday. He wore it and wore it until it was all worn out...except for enough material to make a... (repeat through vest, cap, button).

When you get to button add "it was all worn out...except for enough material left over to make this story which I've shared with you."

Ask the children open-ended comprehension questions such as, Do you think it was the right thing for the tailor to use the leftover material from the suit? Why? How do you think the tailor might be able to acquire beautiful clothes?

SUMMARY

In addition to developing listening skills, this story provides a good way to help children develop an awareness of the less fortunate people in our society and it can be used to inspire the work ethic.

ASSESSMENT

Ask the class to answer comprehension questions about the story, then check the students' answers for feasibility, creativeness, and accuracy.

ENRICHMENT

Use the Internet to do research concerning the number of homeless people in society. Brainstorm ways the children may help homeless people in the neighborhood (collecting money, food, or clothing).

Listening Detectives

Objective

Students will develop better listening habits and identification of sentence parts by answering questions.

MATERIALS
• dry-erase board and markers
• newspapers

PREPARATION
Label five columns on the board: who, what, why, when, and where. Collect enough copies of newspapers so that each child has one.

PROCEDURE
Ask several children to come to the board and demonstrate the activity. As you read a paragraph from the newspaper slowly and distinctly to them, the children should fill in the appropriate column on the board that answers the questions (who, when, why, etc.). After the demonstration, ask each child to choose a paragraph from his or her newspaper and circle the answers to each of the questions. Let children read their paragraphs orally and tell why the part they circled answers the questions. Explain to the children that all well-written stories contain this information.

SUMMARY
This activity helps children develop listening skills as they listen for specific information to complete the columns.

ASSESSMENT

Check the paragraphs for correct form and to determine if the children have included the five Ws.

ENRICHMENT

Children may work with partners to each write a paragraph and then exchange paragraphs with their partners. The partners then circle all the answers to who, what, where, why, and when. Many local newspapers have a Newspaper in Education program that is free to schools. Many larger newspapers that participate in the program have an education coordinator who visits schools and demonstrates the different ways a newspaper can be used to teach skills in all academic areas. Contact your local newspaper about the program.

Vocabulary Express

Objective

The students will increase listening skills and vocabulary through a structured listening activity.

MATERIALS
- different colored construction paper including black for a railroad track
- blank train schedules for each student

PREPARATION

Construct a train with the cars made from different colored construction paper, a black construction paper railroad track that is taped to the classroom wall, and train schedules for all the children. Tape construction paper signs with the names of the places (Here, Wordsville, Vocabulary Station, etc.) at different points on the classroom wall above the railroad track. Begin the train at Here; the destination is There.

PROCEDURE

Begin the train with a new word on the engine and one on the caboose with no cars in between. The "train" words may be a list of vocabulary words from the stories the children will be reading that week in their reading textbooks or from their list of spelling words. Pronounce the words for the children, but do not give them the definitions unless they specifically ask for them. Have the students listen for the words during the day as you use them in context, so they will get an idea of the meaning; or, you may want to give a "built-in" definition. For example, "Some bears hibernate; that is, they sleep during the winter." Alert listeners will recognize the words as "train" words. Each day the train grows as the engine is moved up and two or three cars are added. Soon it will stretch from Here to There!

Let each child keep his or her own train schedule. If children hear the words used, understand their meanings, and/or use them correctly in oral or written communication, they have arrived at a certain point toward their destination: There. For example, if the engine is at Lollipop Place, and the student knows all the words in the train from the engine to the caboose, he or she can mark the arrival date on the schedule.

SUMMARY

This is a good activity to encourage children to listen for a specific purpose. It helps them to understand that listening involves a number of factors such as attention, focusing on the purpose of listening, and responding.

ASSESSMENT

Assess vocabulary growth by administering a vocabulary test using the "train" words.

ENRICHMENT

The teacher can easily integrate math skills into this activity by letting students note departure and arrival times on their train schedules and computing the time it takes them or the distance. This also would be an excellent time for a field trip to a train station. Children may plan trips they would like to take for vacation. The teacher may get actual train schedules from the train station and let children decide on a departure and arrival time to their favorite places (for example, Disney World). They can write about the places they would like to visit and look up information on the Internet.

PART FIVE

Developing the Art of Viewing

In addition to the language arts of reading, writing, speaking, and listening, a fifth language art has been recognized: viewing. In society today, we are constantly being bombarded with visual images to interpret. The information presented on the Internet requires the use of visual interpretation. Television, media, and all types of advertisements use visual images to portray information. In order for children to become literate in interpreting visual representation, they need many experiences to expose them to this type of communication. According to Rubin (2000), "The more activities that students are exposed to that stress the effect that visual messages have for individuals, the better prepared these students will be to live in the twenty first century" (p. 8).

Art is a good medium to use to help children translate ideas, concepts, and experiences through viewing (Schirrmacher, 1993). Gunning (2000) describes another viewing activity as a "text walk," in which the teacher goes through the textbook pointing out illustrations, word formations, charts, etc. that will help the student to comprehend the material. *Standards for the English Language Arts* (IRA/NCTE, 1996) stresses that children be able to use visual language effectively (see Appendix B). Being able to understand graphic representation is related to one of the intelligences identified by Gardner (1994). Gardner's research helps teachers to realize that this is a way of learning for children, and it is the responsibility of the teacher to include activities that promote this type of learning. Viewing the illustrations in a text influences children's comprehension of that text (Tiedt, Tiedt, & Tiedt, 2001). Goldberg (2001) determined that students have a much better understanding of a situation by viewing a painting or picture than they do by simply reading about the situation.

Children need to be taught the importance of viewing as a language art skill and how to apply this skill to visual information they are deluged with each day. Activities in this section are designed to help children acquire this skill.

REFERENCES

Gardner, H. (1994). *Creating minds: An anatomy of creativity seen through the lives of Freud, Einstein, Picasso, Stravinsky, Eliot, Graham, and Ghandi.* New York: Basic Books.

Goldberg, M. (2001). *Arts and learning: An integrated approach to teaching and learning in multicultural and multilingual settings* (2nd ed.). New York: Longman.

Gunning, T.G. (2000). *Best books for building literacy for elementary school children.* Boston: Allyn & Bacon.

Rubin, D. (2000). *Teaching elementary language arts: A balanced approach* (6th ed.). Boston: Allyn & Bacon.

Schirrmacher, R. (1993). *Art and creative development for young children* (2nd ed.). New York: Delmar.

Tiedt, P.L., Tiedt, I.M., & Tiedt, S.W. (2001). *Language arts activities for the classroom* (3rd ed.). Boston: Allyn & Bacon.

Pudding Painting

Objective

*Students will use visual representation
to interpret a poem.*

MATERIALS

- instant vanilla pudding mix
- food coloring
- art paper
- writing materials

PREPARATION

Discuss with the students the importance of interpreting visual
information. For example, ask them how they decide which book
to choose to read (cover? title?). When they are riding down the
road on their bikes, why should they be able to interpret the
meanings of the different signs along the road (stop signs, railroad
crossing, etc.)? When they are in the grocery story, what helps
them decide on a food they want to buy (picture on box, brand
name)? Explain to the students that they are going to be given a
copy of a poem (or you can read a poem to the students) and that
they are to interpret the meaning of that poem by creating a
picture or illustration that indicates the meaning. The students will
create the illustration using pudding mix and art paper. Markers
may be used to add details or signatures to the illustrations.

PROCEDURE

Prepare the vanilla instant pudding. After it is mixed, divide the
pudding into three or four containers. Add different food colors to
each container (red, green, yellow, etc.). Give each student art
paper and three or four containers of the pudding mix. Put the
pudding into small paper cups or bowls for the students. The

students are to use the pudding to finger paint their interpretation of the poem on the art paper. Place the painting on a table to dry. When the paintings are dry, display them in the classroom. These paintings will look good enough to eat!

SUMMARY

This is a fun way to help the students realize the importance of visual representation. By interpreting the poems through visual representation, students increase their comprehension of the poems because they have to think critically about what the author is trying to communicate to them through the poem.

ASSESSMENT

The teacher may assess the students' work by observing the paintings to make sure they accurately interpret a poem's meaning. Note creativity and use of colors and details or lack of details used in the paintings.

ENRICHMENT

Ask the students to construct a Haiku poem and illustrate it. The Haiku is a Japanese poetic form consisting of three lines composed of seventeen syllables, five in the first and third lines and seven in the second.

Page and Screen

Objective

The students will be able to discern the differences in a printed book and a videotape of the story.

MATERIALS

• narrative book such as *Charlotte's Web* and videotape of the story

PREPARATION

Read *Charlotte's Web* by E.B. White to the children. Read a chapter a day until the book is finished. Third-grade children may want to read the book on their own.

PROCEDURE

After you have finished reading the book to the children, let them view the videotape version of the story. This will be available at most video stores, the school library, or the public library. Discuss the differences in the two versions. Which did they enjoy more? Why? Is the book accurately portrayed in the videotape? How do you think the author of the story feels about this portrayal? Should the story be changed without the author's consent? Why?

SUMMARY

This activity helps students become aware of the fact that the same information can be presented differently and that different presentation methods can distort or change the meaning of the original information.

ASSESSMENT

Observe students' responses to questions. Use a checklist to evaluate critical and creative thinking (see Appendix A).

ENRICHMENT

Students can role-play different characters in the story to better understand what the character is feeling. This can be done in small groups and then presented to the class.

Picture This

Objective

The students will increase their observation skills through the use of photographs and will write creatively using information from photographs.

MATERIALS

- transparencies made from photographs depicting various scenes and people (can be printed from the Internet)
- writing materials

PREPARATION

Use the computer to locate various photographs of people or places. Print the photos on transparencies.

PROCEDURE

Show several of the photographs on the transparencies using an overhead projector. Ask students to observe the details of the photographs very carefully. Ask them to write the things they observe in the photographs and questions they have about the photographs. Let students work in small groups to discuss the observations and share ideas. Next, ask the students to choose one of the photographs viewed and write a letter as if they were someone in the photograph, or they may write to someone in the photograph.

SUMMARY

This activity helps the students to learn to recognize details and improve observation skills. It is a good motivator for ideas for creative writing.

ASSESSMENT

Observe students' ability to write creatively using a rubric for creative writing (see Appendix A).

ENRICHMENT

Let the students choose a different photograph of a scene. Ask them to write a poem describing the scene and to include the place they think the scene depicts. The students may locate this place on the map and give directions to the place from their hometown.

Pantomime Party

Objectives

Students will be able to visually recognize characters and sequence from a story through pantomime.

MATERIALS

• familiar narrative stories such as *The Three Bears* by Paul Galdone

PREPARATION

Divide the children into groups of four or five each. Ask each group to read a particular story silently.

PROCEDURE

Discuss the events that happened in the story in sequence. Have the students describe the characters in the story. Ask the students to work in small groups to assign roles of the various characters and to practice pantomiming the characters and the sequence of events that happened in their story. Next, ask each group to pantomime the characters and the sequence of events portrayed in the story for the class. The class is then to identify the characters and the sequence of events.

SUMMARY

This activity provides an opportunity for all students to be successful. By working in small groups, all the students are able to discuss and comprehend the story. Thus, each student is able to portray a character and the sequence of the story successfully.

ASSESSMENT

Use a checklist to assess students' portrayal of the characters (tone of voice, actions, enthusiasm, etc.), social skills (cooperation, sharing, turn-taking, etc.), and knowledge of sequence (see Appendix A for some examples).

ENRICHMENT

Students can work cooperatively to construct a mural depicting the characters and events in a story. They may also create a storyboard by drawing the pictures on a transparency and coloring the pictures with transparency markers. The transparencies then can be projected on a screen for the class to view. Stories may be created to go along with the pictures.

Wildlife Treasure Trek

Objective

Students will be able to describe differences seen in an environment as the result of casual and detailed observations.

MATERIALS

• writing materials and journals

PREPARATION

Discuss with students the importance of viewing literacy. Discuss the fact that they can learn to be more observant by using all their senses, being aware of their surroundings, and recognizing any part of their environment as being part of a larger whole. Cover a large table in the classroom containing supplies, books, and other materials with a sheet before the students arrive.

PROCEDURE

Say to the class, "Let's practice our observation skills," then ask the students to write down all the things that they remember seeing on the table before it was covered. Uncover the table and ask the students to list the things they see. Conduct a class discussion. What kinds of things did they remember? What kinds of things did they miss? Ask students to list reasons why they remembered some things and did not remember other things.

Tell the students that they are going to play a game to see how observant they are called Wildlife Treasure Trek. Remind the students that wildlife includes insects, spiders, reptiles, amphibians, and most species of fish, birds, and mammals. Take the students outside to the school grounds, and divide the class into small groups of four each. Tell each group to pick a spot on the ground to observe for 15 minutes. Give them a list of things they are to look for: evidence that humans and wildlife share environments, wildlife is all around us, wildlife ranges in size, and both people and wildlife need places to live. Tell the students to be careful and not to kill any wildlife or damage their homes. Ask them to record in their journals the evidence they observe. Return to the classroom and compare results of the observations.

SUMMARY

This activity helps students to understand the importance of conservation and that people and wildlife share environments. It also is a good way to integrate science and social studies.

ASSESSMENT

Check the children's journals for the number of items they have observed and the entry for grammatical errors. If assigning a grade, add points to the grade for creative writing such as assigning human characteristics to animals they observe. A checklist may be used to check group participation.

ENRICHMENT

You may add other things to the list for the students to observe. The list may be used for students to conduct a scavenger hunt. Also, students may compile the information they gathered, and construct a graph showing this information. For example, the graph may show the different types of wildlife, sizes of the wildlife, and evidence that we share the same environment.

PART SIX

Learning the Importance of Visually Representing

Goldberg (2001) states that representation is a critical element of learning, and describes the importance of using the arts as a way of visually representing information in all subject areas. An activity she recommends for teaching visual representation is to teach cursive writing through the use of dance. Through dance, the students are introduced to curves and motions with their bodies. Another activity she recommends to teach spelling and vocabulary is "picto-spelling" (p. 34), which involves incorporating words into a descriptive picture. Students put the letters of the word together in such a way that they form a picture of the word. Drama is another way Goldberg describes incorporating visual representation. Through drama, students are able to experience the roles of the characters and gain a better insight into their feelings. Rubin (2000) discusses the importance of how the electronic age in which we live mandates the ability to understand and use visual representation. Students are now being taught to create Web pages and slide shows using the computer.

Students should learn to create graphic organizers to better understand concepts and to clearly present information to others. When students create a graphic organizer such as a story web (Hennings, 1994; Pappas, Kiefer, & Levstik, 1998), it activates their schemas and helps them to better understand the story. To better communicate results of an experiment or oral report, students should be able to visually represent the findings using posters, collages, pictures, and images created with a computer (Abruscato, 2000). Use of visual images is an excellent means of connecting the cognitive and affective dimensions of literacy (Collins-Block, 2001).

Although visually representing is a recent addition to the language arts, it is becoming more and more important as society continues to rely on visual representation to communicate ideas, concepts, and other information. The activities presented in this section will help students to enhance their skills of visually representing information.

REFERENCES

Abruscato, J. (2000). *Teaching children science: A discovery approach* (5th ed.). Boston: Allyn & Bacon.

Collins-Block, C. (2001). *Teaching the language arts: Expanding thinking through student-centered instruction* (3rd ed.). Boston: Allyn & Bacon.

Goldberg, M. (2001). *Arts and learning: An integrated approach to teaching and learning in multicultural and multilingual settings* (2nd ed.). New York: Longman.

Hennings, D.G. (1994). *Communication in action: Teaching the language arts* (5th ed.). New York: Houghton Mifflin.

Pappas, C.C., Kiefer, B.Z., & Levstik, L.S. (1999). *An integrated language perspective in the elementary school: An action approach* (3rd ed.). Reading, MA: Addison-Wesley.

Rubin, D. (2000). *Teaching elementary language arts: A balanced approach* (6th ed.). Boston: Allyn & Bacon.

Circular Stories

Objective

The students will be able to develop understanding of the circular story format by creating a circular, sequential graphic organizer for the story.

MATERIALS
- marker board or large sheet of paper
- markers
- tape
- story by Laura Numeroff such as *If You Give a Pig a Pancake* with accompanying story cards (you can scan scenes from the book depicting the sequence and print the scenes using a computer or list the different parts of the story on index cards)
- paper and pencils

PREPARATION
Draw a large circle on the board or on paper. Discuss the difference between a linear story and a circular story. In the circular story, each part calls for something else such as when you give a pig a pancake, she's going to want some syrup. When you give a pig some syrup, she's going to want some butter, etc. Each thing calls for something else until you get to the end of the story and the ending goes back to the beginning. A linear story has a beginning, middle, and end and doesn't go in a circle.

PROCEDURE
Read *If You Give a Pig a Pancake* to the class. Discuss why the story is considered circular. Show the students the pictures or cards depicting the sequence of the story, and ask them to put the cards in the order that they happened. Let the students tape the cards in order around the large circle you drew. Give students the prompt

"If you give a _____ a _____" (using an animal and a food item). Divide the class into groups of four and ask the students to create their own circle stories using the prompt. Tell them to create a graphic organizer by listing the events in the story in sequence using the circle example you showed them earlier. Allow the different groups to share their stories orally with the class.

SUMMARY

This exercise helps students acquire comprehension skills by having them remember the sequence of events in a story. It is an excellent way to introduce the concept of cause and effect. A story web can be used in place of the circle to develop a graphic organizer.

ASSESSMENT

Evaluate students' ability to create an accurate graphic organizer, and evaluate their original stories to determine whether or not they understand the concept of a circular story, that is, that the stories end in the same place they began and have logical connections between events. This can be assessed through observation by using a checklist.

ENRICHMENT

The students can illustrate their stories by creating their own story cards and a circular graphic organizer. They can exchange their finished products with their classmates and have fun playing the "circle game." The cards can be placed on clothes hangers using paper clips to create mobiles to hang in the classroom.

Picture Perfect

Objective

The students will expand and add variety to their spelling and writing vocabulary.

MATERIALS
- dry-erase board
- poster paper
- crayons, paints, and markers
- writing materials
- small boxes such as shoeboxes

PREPARATION
Arrange the materials and tell the students they are going to paint a colorful picture with words instead of paint. Explain to them that a writer uses words to create pictures in our minds, which is what the children will attempt to do. For example, give students the sentence *The boy could see the sunrise.* Then add this to the sentence: *The boy could see a brilliant sunrise with all the colors of the rainbow shining through the clouds.* Next, ask which sentence helps them to see the sun rise more clearly in their minds. Explain that you have painted a picture using words.

PROCEDURE
Begin by writing a word on the board such as *sunset.* Ask students to brainstorm as many words as they can to describe it or how they feel about it. These words can then compose one week's spelling lesson. The class should next write a story that uses these words. The children should illustrate the story and cut out the illustrations, then glue the illustrations inside the shoeboxes to create dioramas.

SUMMARY

This activity creates an attractive display of the students' work for the classroom, and it serves as a good review for the spelling words.

ASSESSMENT

Use a rubric to judge the stories according to originality or creativeness (see Appendix A).

ENRICHMENT

The stories may be made into a book to be placed in the classroom reading area.

Mural Game

Objective

The students will develop retention and recall of information by painting a mural and describing the characters.

MATERIALS
- storybooks
- bulletin board paper
- paints

PREPARATION
Arrange the materials so students have a large space (for example, the floor of the classroom) for completing the mural.

PROCEDURE
Have the students read an assigned story. Tell them that they are going to play a game afterward about the characters and the background in the story, so they should remember as many details as they can. After the students read the story they should put the story material away. Using the bulletin board paper that has been spread on the carpet, tell the students that each one is to make a part of a mural. Assign characters and, one by one, have students draw the character or object and tell about it (for example, "I'm Janet; I have yellow hair; and I run in the story." Or, "I'm a tree; I move in the wind; and I'm old and tall"). Students get a point for each item they can tell about the story. The winner is the student with the most points.

SUMMARY

You may divide the class into small groups. Select a leader for each group and let the leader assign different character roles to group members. The students role-play the different characters for the class, and the class guesses which story the characters are in.

ASSESSMENT

Assess the students' recall of the information by using a checklist. Group participation and social skills also may be evaluated using a checklist (see Appendix A).

ENRICHMENT

The students may use the murals as stage decorations for the story and dramatize the story for the class. Other classes may be invited to view the production.

Johnny Appleseed

Objectives

*The students will be able to make a bar graph
and use it to locate information.*

MATERIALS

- the story "Johnny Appleseed"
- construction paper
- paints
- writing materials
- scissors
- tape
- foam meat trays or paper plates
- apples cut into halves
- tempera paint (red, green, and yellow)

PREPARATION

Have students read "Johnny Appleseed." Discuss the events in the story and talk about how Johnny Appleseed made many friends through his travels. Draw a large bar graph on the board or on a transparency using an overhead projector.

PROCEDURE

Tell the students they are to construct a bar graph using the theme "apples." Remind them of Johnny Appleseed's journey and the different types of apples mentioned in the story. Pass a basket around the classroom containing different color apples (cut from construction paper). Ask each student to select his or her favorite "type" of apple, and let each student tape the apple in the appropriate column of the bar graph drawn on the board. Ask the students to read the information from the graph such as, What is the class favorite apple? Why do you think this apple is the favorite? What is the least favorite? If you owned a grocery store how would this information help you in deciding which apples to stock in your store? Next, ask the students to construct their own bar graphs using paper and paints. Let students volunteer to share their graphs with the class. The students then may ask other students in the class questions concerning the information the graphs show.

SUMMARY

This activity helps students understand graphic information by personalizing a bar graph. It gives them practice in reading information from the graph and in constructing graphs. This is a good way to integrate math, science, and social studies into language arts.

ASSESSMENT

Assess the students' ability to read information from graphs by constructing a written test that contains questions that can be answered from reading the information on the graph. For example, ask the students which apples they most prefer or least prefer.

ENRICHMENT

Apple prints can be made by cutting apples into halves and dipping them into different colored paints (paints should be poured into paper plates for dipping the apples). Next place the apple on white construction paper. The apple prints can be combined in different ways to make interesting pictures. Cut out large apple shapes from red and green construction paper to make covers for apple booklets. Place writing paper between the covers and staple together. These can be made into poetry booklets, story booklets, or journals. The children also can help make applesauce.

Objectives

The students will develop an awareness and respect for different cultures by noting likenesses and differences in all people.

MATERIALS

- writing materials
- paints
- construction paper
- magazines

PREPARATION

Discuss the differences in cultures. Tell students that the United States has a large amount of school-age children from different countries. Because these students are different and new they may experience feelings of alienation, rejection, and isolation. Discuss ways the students may help these new students feel at home (learning about their cultures, families, etc.).

PROCEDURE

The class can brainstorm attributes that all people have in common. Give the students an assignment to interview their parents and grandparents or guardians. Students should ask what country their ancestors came from originally, what were some of the customs, what holidays were celebrated, what were some of their favorite foods, etc. After the students have collected this information, have them construct posters showing the information. They should orally share the information with the class. As they share the information they should locate on a world map where their ancestors came from and use the poster to visually represent the information.

SUMMARY

Through the visual representations of the posters and maps, the students are able to see likenesses and differences in the cultures. This activity helps them to develop an awareness and respect of different cultures.

ASSESSMENT

Construct a written test to assess students' knowledge of different cultures. An attitude survey also may be used.

ENRICHMENT

Have the class work in cooperative groups to make a collage depicting the theme "We Are the World." Pictures representing diverse groups of people can be cut from magazines and glued together to make the collage.

PART SEVEN

Applying Cooperative Learning Strategies Through Creative Dramatics

Creative teachers have long been using dramatics in their classrooms as imaginative learning activities to develop their students' language skills. From impromptu skits to creative dramatics and theatrical display, children have been learning communication skills in exciting, active environments (Goldberg, 2001). It is in this kind of activity that children use all their language skills because they speak with expression, listen, read their parts, and write their scripts. Creative dramatics should never be considered a frill, but a valuable learning strategy for all subject areas (Schirrmacher, 1993). For example, these activities can be used as a vehicle to integrate social studies, science, and mathematics concepts (Day, 1994; Jarrett, 1997). Rowe (1998) concludes that through role-playing, students are able to symbolically transform both role relationships and objects in order to explore the world through the perspectives of authors and their characters.

There are other ancillary benefits to using dramatics in your classroom. By the nature of dramatics, people interact socially, and these experiences of mingling and cooperating facilitate the acquisition of social skills such as getting along with others and respecting each person's personal worth (Schirrmacher, 1993).

In this section you will find dramatic activities to help you set the stage for communication skill development. Your students will enthusiastically immerse themselves in these activities because children by nature are expressive and take delight in projecting their personalities (Rubin, 2000). Shy, reserved students will have many opportunities to learn that satisfaction is derived from open expression.

All the activities offered here may be conducted using cooperative learning groups. According to Johnson and Johnson (1999), cooperative learning benefits include better problem-solving skills, higher achievement, higher self-esteem, and improved interpersonal relationships. Students may work in cooperative learning groups to construct puppets and present puppet shows, write plays, role-play, and act out different characters. Once your students are involved in these activities, their enthusiastic participation will reveal that dramatic activity is an effective language-learning vehicle.

REFERENCES

Day, B. (1994). *Early childhood education: Developmental/experiential teaching and learning* (4th ed.). New York: Macmillan.

Goldberg, M. (2001). *Arts and learning: An integrated approach to teaching and learning in multicultural and multilingual settings* (2nd ed.). New York: Longman.

Jarrett, O.S. (1997). Science activities. *The Elementary School Classroom, 34*(2), 13–27.

Johnson, D.W., & Johnson, R.T. (1999). Making cooperative learning work. *Theory Into Practice, 38*(2), 67–73.

Rowe, D.W. (1998). The literate potentials of book-related dramatic play. *Reading Research Quarterly, 33,* 10–36.

Rubin, D. (2000). *Teaching elementary language arts: A balanced approach* (6th ed.). Boston: Allyn & Bacon.

Schirrmacher, R. (1993). *Art and creative development for young children* (2nd ed.). New York: Delmar.

Readers Theatre

Objective

The students will develop creative expression through a Readers Theatre presentation.

MATERIALS
• selected novels, poetry books, and duplicate copies of stories or poems

PREPARATION
Explain that Readers Theatre is an activity in which the students select a favorite story from a book and read the story as they sit on chairs in front of the class. Divide the class into groups. They may use books from the classroom selection or get books from the library. After the stories are chosen, make copies for each student in the group. Arrange a row of chairs in front of the classroom.

PROCEDURE
Let the students work together in groups to choose the story they want to present in the activity. Give each student a copy of the story. Tell them to practice reading the story in their groups, and to assign each person a part of the story or character dialogue to read. They may select poems or narratives to read. They can be creative and use actions to accompany the reading. Ask each group to do the production sitting in the chairs in front of the class (or standing in front of the class to do the actions).

SUMMARY
This activity motivates students to read and aids comprehension. Comprehension is aided by setting a purpose for reading (sharing and acting out the different stories in the groups). Students are motivated to understand the story because they want to perform well.

ASSESSMENT

Assess social skills such as cooperation, sharing, and respect for others using a checklist or rubric (see Appendix A).

ENRICHMENT

Choose a period in U.S. history such as the Civil War and let the students role-play the different characters to get the feeling of what it was like during this time. Ask them to evaluate the period and tell what may have been done differently.

Animal Antics

Objective

The students will develop positive self-concepts and respect for others by playing a game using comparison of animal traits.

MATERIALS

- typed description of each character's traits along with a cut-out of each animal character that is portraying a human personality trait

PREPARATION

Explain to the students that everyone is unique and different, and that this is what makes each person special. Explain that because a person is different doesn't mean that he or she is bad.

PROCEDURE

Students will act out different character types in the form of a game. Each student picks a character (with description and dialogue attached) and will act out his or her part independently of, but within, the total group. Start the lesson by asking the students if they have ever wanted to be someone or something else. Discuss what the children feel like at that moment. Then have 10 volunteers come forward and each student pick an animal character (with human traits) at random and each student act out his or her specific part (for example, a chipmunk with an allergy, a shy mouse, a blind mole, a crippled rabbit).

SUMMARY

This is a good way to help students develop an awareness and appreciation of diversity. It helps them to realize the difficulties handicapped people face.

ASSESSMENT

Assess this activity by observation of student participation and student attitudinal changes.

ENRICHMENT

The students can work in small groups to discuss ways they can be of assistance to other handicapped students. They can use the Internet to look up information on different types of handicaps caused by certain diseases.

Paper Bag Production

Objective

The students will develop oral communication skills
by creating and sharing a story.

MATERIALS

- five or six large paper bags containing five or six items each
- additional paper bags to use for puppets
- markers
- yarn
- construction paper
- glue

PREPARATION

Divide the class into cooperative learning groups of four or five each.

PROCEDURE

The groups will take 5 minutes to create a story in which they would use each of the articles contained in the paper bag. (More time may be given depending on the groups' progression.) The bag may contain such things as pieces of velvet cloth, buttons, toy soldiers, or caps. The story may be something like "A velveteen rabbit (cloth) lost his eye (button) while playing with the soldier (toy). The boy (cap) helps the rabbit find the lost eye." Next the group should construct puppets (rabbit, toy, cap) to use when presenting the story to the class. Each group will perform its production for the rest of the class while practicing good communication skills (using complete sentences, correct subject/verb agreement, etc.).

SUMMARY

This activity gives the students an opportunity to practice oral communication by working together cooperatively as a group. Students learn language use by talking among themselves.

ASSESSMENT

Use a checklist to record each child's use of oral language (see Appendix A). Look for use of complete sentences, subject/verb agreement, and correct use of plurals.

ENRICHMENT

The groups may make paper-bag puppets using the art supplies. They may write a story and present it to the class as a puppet show.

Peek Box Brainstorm

Objective

The students will develop oral expression and creative thinking by using a peek box to tell a story.

MATERIALS

- shoebox
- different small objects
- tape recorder

PREPARATION

Construct a "peek box" by placing several objects inside a shoebox. Example objects to place in the peek box may be a cotton ball, a scrap of material, tiny toys such as animals or cars, yarn, etc. Choose objects that students can weave a story around. Cut a small hole in the box for students to peek through to see the objects.

PROCEDURE

Place the peek box in the listening center so that individual students can observe the objects in the peek box. Place it on a table next to a tape recorder. Individual students will peek into the box and, with the recorder on, tell a story about the objects in the box. Students' stories should include as many of the objects in the box as possible. Students can then listen to their stories and share them with the class. The teacher may choose to let all the students complete this activity or may use this activity selectively with students who need practice with their oral language skills.

SUMMARY

This helps the teacher detect language errors and gives students the opportunity to use oral language.

ASSESSMENT

Assess the oral expression by noting errors in the students' language. Creative thinking can be assessed using a rubric to judge originality and innovative ideas in the story (see Appendix A).

ENRICHMENT

The students can work in cooperative learning groups to dramatize the story. The students may also write and illustrate the stories they create. The stories can be compiled into a book, which can be left in the listening center with the tapes. Students may then listen to the tape-recorded stories and read along with the tapes as they look at the books. Listening to the tapes as they read along will help students pronounce unknown words in the stories.

Goofies

Objective

*The students will learn creative expression through
the use of humorous poetry.*

MATERIALS

- poems such as "Eletephony," "Kangarooster," "Octopussy," or
  any other article about an animal in a different fashion than it is
  usually thought of
- paper
- pencil
- crayons

PREPARATION

Read the poems or stories to the students to introduce the lesson.
Discuss with them why these animals' names are "goofy" and
how other foolish names can be created.

PROCEDURES

Direct students to create, draw, and color their own goofies and
to give them names. Provide a time to let the students share their
original drawings. After they have completed this activity, tell them
to name their goofies and during free time to write a story or
poem to accompany them. Students will work in groups to
practice acting out their stories. The group will choose one story
to act out for the class. Explain that a book titled *Our Big Book of
Goofies* will be made for the reading table and each person in
the class will put his or her favorite goofie story in the book when
it's completed.

SUMMARY

Children enjoy this activity because they love silly poems and funny animals. They also enjoy being able to create their own "goofy" animals and having their stories included in a class book. The students value their work and by including their work in a class book you are showing them that you also value their work, which is a good way to enhance their self-concepts.

ASSESSMENT

Using a rubric or checklist, the teacher may assess the stories according to creativity and correct use of oral language (see Appendix A).

ENRICHMENT

The book the students construct may be laminated and bound, and a copy can be placed in the school library. Stories also may be submitted to publishers of children's work (see Appendix D).

PART EIGHT

Gaining Competency in Computer Applications

Teachers today must possess the ability to use instructional technology, especially computer-based technologies. As Rafferty (1999) notes, "Computers have enormous potential as teaching and learning tools, but they require users to learn declarative (the what), procedural (the how), and conditional (the when, where, why and under what circumstances) knowledge" (p. 23). Abdal-Haqq (1995) discusses the following factors that require teachers to use instructional technology in their classes: Teachers need to provide relevant and authentic instruction that reflects society, meets student and parent expectations concerning instructional technology, and meets federal, state, and district mandates related to the use of instructional technology.

There are numerous ways teachers can use instructional technology in the classrooms today. Barclay and York (1999) describe the use of e-mail as an alternative to paper and pencil assessments. They explain that this method measures students' abilities to set priorities, make decisions, and organize information. Written communication through technology is an innovative way to teach writing skills (McKay, 1998). As students become familiar with operating the computer, they also can become familiar with basic editing functions such as the thesaurus and spell check.

Reading comprehension can be improved using the World Wide Web (Lewin, 1999). Students are highly motivated to read Web sites, so using this motivation to teach students how to read the Web or "site read" can improve reading skills.

Research using the Internet is another important way to use technology in the classroom. In teaching a unit on volcanoes, the question may arise, Which volcano eruption did the most destruction? This can easily be found using the Internet. There are numerous software programs available that will help you integrate technology instruction into the language arts. Many times teachers are hesitant to use technology instruction because they feel it will be either too difficult or too time consuming for themselves and their students. The following teacher-friendly activities will help to overcome this hesitancy.

REFERENCES

Abdal-Haqq, I. (1995). Infusing technology into preservice teacher education. *ERIC Digest, 94*(6).

Barclay, L.A., & York, K.M. (1999). Electronic communication skills in the classroom: An e-mail in-basket exercise. *Journal of Education for Business, 74*(4), 249.

Lewin, L. (1999). Site-reading the World Wide Web. *Educational Leadership, 56*(5), 16–20.

McKay, M.D. (1998). Technology and language arts: Great support for every classroom! *Book Report, 17*(3), 3.

Rafferty, C.D. (1999). Literacy in the information age. *Educational Leadership, 57*(2), 22–25.

Weather on the Web

Objectives

The students will correctly display the daily forecast each morning after they research a weather report using the Internet.

MATERIALS

- large, laminated map of your state or province
- dry-erase markers
- computer with Internet access
- three-pronged folders for each student
- graph chart

PREPARATION

Display the map and graph somewhere in the room that will be accessible for the students. Assign students to small groups of five each. (A group will be selected each week to perform weather forecast duties.) All the students will keep a weather journal by placing pages in the three-pronged folder.

PROCEDURE

At the beginning of each week identify a group to research the weather, place weather symbols on the map, and graph information for the week. Each morning have the group research the day's forecast on the Internet and then use the dry-erase markers to draw the weather symbol for the day on the laminated map. (Example: If it is going to be sunny all day, then only the sun will be needed.) The group will also graph the forecasts on the graph chart each day of the week. Have all the students write the day's forecast and a prediction for tomorrow's forecast in their weather journal. The prediction can be based on research or by simply guessing. At the end of the week students can compare their predictions to the weather graph the group has charted. You might consider the following Web sites for the class's research:

http://www.intellicast.com/weather/msp
http://www.rainorshine.com/weather/index/sites/njo
http://www.wapt.com/weather

SUMMARY

This activity includes practice in writing, speaking, viewing, and visually representing. Weather forecasting can be a fun activity for students because weather is something that they have observed and will continue to observe throughout their lifetime. This lesson will introduce students to weather vocabulary and symbols that will enable them to read a weather map and predict a forecast.

ASSESSMENT

The weather journal can be taken up at the end of each week to check for complete sentences, correct grammar, and correct punctuation.

ENRICHMENT

Have the students chart or graph the number of correct predictions they made. They may create their own weather symbols.

Project Planet

Objective

The students will research a planet in the solar system, construct a model of the planet, and give an oral report.

MATERIALS

- writing materials
- computer
- art supplies (Styrofoam balls of various sizes, paints, yarn, Styrofoam cones)
- reference books, encyclopedias, and science textbooks
- construction paper

PREPARATION

Open the discussion with the question, Do you think there is life on any of the other planets? Follow this with a K-W-L (What I Know, What I Want to Know, and What I Learned) chart (Ogle, 1986) about the solar system. The students, with partners, will choose a planet to research. You and the students will decide what topics to cover in the research and at the end of the unit you will create a chart displaying the information.

PROCEDURE

The students will choose the topic to research and use the reference materials and the Internet to write their report. They will then construct a model of the planet using the art supplies. When the reports have been given orally, the students will paint their planet and display it from the ceiling using the yarn. You might consider the following Web sites for the class's research:

http://encarta.msn.com/find/search.asp?search=solar=system
http://encarta.msn.com/alexandra/templates/
      lessonful.asp?page=1560
http://www.solarviews.com/eng/edu/index.htm

SUMMARY

Students enjoy using the Internet to locate information. Combining the research with an art project (constructing the planet model) strengthens the students' comprehension and helps them to remember the information.

ASSESSMENT

The written reports can be checked for grammatical errors and the accuracy of the research. Communication skills can be assessed by listening to the students' oral reports.

ENRICHMENT

Artistic students may make a brochure of the solar system. Education compact discs on the solar system are a good source for remedial instruction in identifying the planets.

REFERENCE

Ogle, D. (1986). K-W-L: A teaching model that develops active reading of expository text. *The Reading Teacher, 39,* 564–570.

Me Poems

Objective

The students will create an autobiographical poem according to specific guidelines.

MATERIALS

- autobiographical poem guidelines
- computer
- colored computer paper
- construction paper
- glue

PREPARATION

Give the students the following autobiographical guidelines:

Line 1: Use your full name as the title; Line 2: Write your first name; Line 3: Describe your appearance (hair color, height, etc.); Line 4: Tell three things you like about yourself (appearance, personality, character traits, etc.); Line 5: Describe three things you would change about yourself; Line 6: Describe three activities you enjoy; Line 7: Describe three things you have experienced (fear, frustration, success, etc.); Line 8: List three things you would like to do in your life; Line 9: Describe three things that made you extremely happy; Line 10: Write your last name.

Tell the students that they will write their own autobiographical poem using the computer and following the guidelines. Determine which word-processing format will be used, and prepare a step-by-step instruction sheet for the students to follow in setting up the format on the computer.

PROCEDURE

Discuss the concept of the autobiography with the students. Stress the difference between biography and the autobiography. Model the guidelines by sharing your own autobiographical poem with the class, and discuss how the poem reveals aspects of your personality to the reader. Explain to the students that the poem will help them to become acquainted with their classmates and help them to become a community, working together and helping each other. The students should complete their poems using the computer, which may take several class periods. When all students have completed their poems, ask each student to orally share his or her poem with the class. Frame the poems by gluing them onto the construction paper, and place the framed poems on the bulletin board.

SUMMARY

This is a good activity to enhance self-esteem and a good introductory activity to use at the beginning of the school year. Compiling the poems into a class book gives the teacher a good record of his or her students from year to year.

ASSESSMENT

Use a rubric to determine if students followed the guidelines to write the autobiographical poem. Check the poem for grammatical errors. Ask students to correct the mistakes before framing the poems and putting them on the bulletin board. Use a checklist to record oral communication skills as the students share their poems with the class (see Appendix A).

ENRICHMENT

Each year the teacher can compile the poems the students write, laminate the pages, place them in a three-ring binder, or the pages may be bound to make a class book. Show students examples of previous class books.

Max's Math Adventures

Objectives

The students will apply math skills to solve problems, find mathematical problems in everyday situations, use creative thinking to find solutions to problems, and use an interactive online form.

MATERIALS

- poem "Max's Fantastical Zoo" by Dan Greenberg
- chart paper
- crayons
- writing materials
- activity sheet printouts

PREPARATION

Locate the Web site http://teacher.scholastic.com. Go to Online Activities and choose Max's Math Adventures. Make copies of the activity sheet printout from the computer. Print the poem "Max's Fantastical Zoo" on a transparency. Project the poem on a large screen or wall or enlarge it and place it on a poster to be displayed in the classroom.

PROCEDURE

Read the poem aloud with the students. Help them identify the math problem that Max and Ruthie are posing as well as the relevant information provided in the poem. Discuss possible solutions to Max's challenge, and explore creative solutions to real-world problems. List the solutions on a chart. As a class, decide on one solution from the list and insert and submit your class's solution using the online form. Read Max's response aloud to the class. If the students' solution is incorrect, you may need to spend an additional class period reviewing the poem and the challenge. Distribute copies of the activity page for students to complete.

SUMMARY

Max's Math Adventures is a math and language arts game created for students in Kindergarten through Grade 2. Each adventure focuses on one math skill integral to the math curriculum. Max and Ruthie challenge young students to solve real-world math problems by using clues embedded in a fun, rhyming poem. Students receive immediate feedback from Max.

ASSESSMENT

To assess critical-thinking skills, ask students to circle the "clue words" they used in the poem to solve Max's challenge. To assess problem solving, ask students to explain how the activity relates to their own lives. Ask students to write a real-world math problem.

ENRICHMENT

Have students make up their own animal for the Fantastical Zoo. Choose a shape that was not used before such as a trapezoid or a hexagon. Describe the animal using as many geometric words as you can.

In Other Words...

Objective

The students will identify and correct grammatical errors in specified paragraphs and use the computer thesaurus to substitute more descriptive language in the same paragraphs.

MATERIALS

- writing materials
- computer
- *The Talking Eggs* by Robert San Souci
- photocopied rewritten selection from the book
- ungrammatical version of selection on the board "as is"
- crayons
- dry-erase board and markers

PREPARATION

Read aloud a selection from *The Talking Eggs*. Have students dictate a list of the descriptive words from the story as you write them on the board. Discuss how the words painted pictures in the mind, then erase the words.

PROCEDURE

Pass out a short selection written to contain grammatical errors and plain nouns or dull adjectives or verbs (underlined). Have the children divide into cooperative groups to edit the selection and make substitutions to make the passage more descriptive. Explain that each group should (1) read each sentence aloud together; (2) discuss the corrections and make the appropriate editing marks; (3) brainstorm to choose silly, serious, realistic, or imaginary substitutions for the underlined words; (4) move to the next sentence and do the same procedure; and (5) choose a group member to read the finished product to the class. As the groups are working on the selection, take one group at a time to the computer to introduce the thesaurus in the word-processing program.

When students have completed editing, rewriting, and illustrating the selection, edit the selection on the board as the students direct you. Then have the designated student from each group read his or her group's version of the selection. Discuss what might have happened to the little boy. Encourage students to talk about how they would have felt. When all the versions have been presented, discuss the advantages of having other people help come up with the ideas. Introduce the concept of the thesaurus as another person with ideas to share.

SUMMARY

In this activity, students engage in group work that heightens interest in material presented and encourages interaction. The students are engaged in the important reinforcement of grammar as well as introduced to the advantages of writing on a computer and using the thesaurus.

ASSESSMENT

Use a checklist to record social skills for the group work. Check the paragraphs for grammatical errors. Check the students' use of the thesaurus by noting the number of descriptive words added to the paragraph.

ENRICHMENT

Have the students write a "blah" story for a partner to embellish.

PART NINE

Working With Literacy Portfolios

Portfolios come in many sizes, shapes, and forms. They serve various purposes and may be used for any and all subject areas. Some are considered working portfolios, which contain a student's work in progress. Others are called showcase portfolios, which contain a student's completed work. Portfolios are being used by kindergarten through college students, and are used to assess preservice and inservice teachers. The type of portfolio used depends on the purpose of the teacher. Whichever type you choose to use, portfolios are considered an excellent means of assessment because they are considered to be an authentic assessment—an alternative to standardized testing. They allow students to have a part in assessment through self-evaluation and reflection.

The assessment portfolio contains samples of children's work collected over a period of time. By examining the samples of work that were completed over a certain time period, the teacher is better able to determine the child's progress and achievement (Meisels & Steele, 1991). The decisions as to what to include in the portfolio should involve the teacher, students, and in some cases the parents. Information from various sources systematically collected over time should be included. Including examples of students' writing in various stages over a period of time provides the teacher with a good means of determining progress and strengths and weaknesses (Rubin, 2000). Grace and Shores (1992) found that using an assessment portfolio helped teachers and students to be more flexible in planning activities that promote physical, affective, social, emotional, and cognitive development. Vukelich (1997) found that portfolios helped teachers to obtain meaningful information about students' literacy development. Another benefit of portfolio assessment is that it helps students to become more responsible by providing them with opportunities to choose work for their portfolios, observations, or any other activity (Culbertson & Jalongo, 1999). The report submitted to the National Education Goals Panel by the Goal One Early Childhood Assessment Resource Group (1999) offers that assessment should be beneficial, valid and reliable, age-appropriate in content and methods, and "should be linguistically appropriate, recognizing that, to some extent, all assessments are measures of language" (p. 36).

In summary, a portfolio is an authentic assessment device that aids teachers in measuring students' progress and determining students' strengths and weaknesses. The following activities provide ways portfolios can be used in language arts.

REFERENCES

Culbertson, L.D., & Jalong, M.R. (1999). But what's wrong with letter grades? *Childhood Education, 75,* 130–135.

Early Childhood Assessment Group. (1999). Principles and recommendations for early childhood assessments. *Early Childhood Today, 13*(5), 35–36.

Grace, C., & Shores, E. (1992). *The portfolio and its use: Developmentally appropriate assessment of young children.* Little Rock, AR: Southern Association on Children.

Meisels, S.J., & Steele, D.E. (1991). *The early childhood portfolio collection process.* Ann Arbor, MI: Center for Human Growth and Development, University of Michigan.

Rubin, D. (2000). *Teaching elementary language arts: A balanced approach* (6th ed.). Boston: Allyn & Bacon.

Vukelich, C. (1997). Assessing young children's literacy: Documenting growth and informing practice. *The Reading Teacher, 50,* 430–434.

Worm Painting

Objectives

The students will locate information on the earthworm, write a report, present it orally in class, and create a worm painting to illustrate the report.

MATERIALS

- reference books or Internet access
- writing materials
- four different colors of food coloring (red, yellow, green, blue)
- meat trays
- plastic forks
- paper towels
- container of earthworms
- white construction paper

PREPARATION

Purchase earthworms from fish bait shop. Arrange other materials as needed.

PROCEDURE

Tell the students that human survival depends in part on the lowly earthworm because the earthworm is essential to the food chain. The earthworm makes soil light, airy, and rich in nutrients so that plants can grow. Animals depend on plants to survive, and humans depend on plants and animals to survive. For additional information on the importance of the earthworm, have the students read *Wonderful Worms* by Linda Glasser. Ask them to do research using the references available and to write a report on the earthworm. Tell them the reports will be presented orally when everyone finishes.

When the reports are finished, tell students that they are going to make a worm painting. Mix a small amount of water with each food coloring in the meat tray. Put a worm in each color until the worm is well colored (this isn't harmful to the earthworms). Place the worms on construction paper and allow them to move freely and make designs on the paper. Use worms of all four colors to complete the design. Students should add titles to the worm paintings. Allow paintings to dry and mount them on the marker tray of the dry-erase board. Return the worms to their environment and discuss the importance of respecting life.

SUMMARY

Through this activity, the students use reading, writing, speaking, listening, and viewing skills, and the activity integrates language arts, science, social studies, and art.

ASSESSMENT

Use a rubric to evaluate the written and oral reports (see Appendix A).

ENRICHMENT

The students may display the worm paintings by creating an art gallery in the hall of the school or in the school library. The students may select judges to judge the paintings. The teacher may use the computer to create award certificates for paintings judged first, second, and third places.

The students may also start a worm farm. Place several earthworms in a glass container such as an aquarium that has been filled loosely with soil. Students should use the Internet to research earthworms. For food, mix the following ingredients and place in the worm farm: ½ cup oatmeal, ½ cup ground coffee, and 1 tablespoon milk. The students should observe the earthworms daily, and should keep a journal describing the activities of the earthworms.

Objective

Students will use expressive and figurative language to create vivid stories with a beginning, middle, and end.

MATERIALS

- writing materials including crayons or a computer with Storybook Weaver software

PREPARATION

After reading any piece of children's literature, discuss with the students the different parts of the story. Then use a story wheel or web and record the story. Next, ask students to brainstorm in small groups about a topic that relates to the story. Students should record their brainstorming ideas on the wheel or web.

PROCEDURE

After brainstorming and recording their ideas, ask students to group the ideas that fit together by circling them with different color crayons. Next, ask students to write about their topic using these ideas. Remind them that good stories have a beginning, middle, and end. Next, students should edit and revise their stories with a friend. Last, students may go to the computer to publish their work using the Storybook Weaver program (available from The Learning Company). If the program isn't available, the stories can be written and illustrated. The stories will be printed and bound as a book for the class library.

SUMMARY

Storybook Weaver gives students an opportunity to publish and share their work with others. Often these are the only books that children have to read at home. Storybook weaving also is an effective way to nurture students' writing and allow it to grow.

ASSESSMENT

Allow students to help you make a scoring rubric for the writing assignments (see Appendix A) after explaining the criteria for the project. Place the corrected stories in the portfolio.

ENRICHMENT

Compile individual stories into a collection for a class anthology of students' work on a particular topic. Encourage students to check out the anthology to read with parents and family. Send a journal with the class anthology when it is checked out, and ask students and parents to write comments about the anthology in the journal.

Character Creation

Objective

The students will increase comprehension and language skills through recalling and sharing stories.

MATERIALS
- art materials such as construction paper, paints, and yarn
- writing materials
- narrative books

PREPARATION

Ask students to read a favorite story silently. Tell them to remember the character descriptions and details in the story. Tell them that they will create a character book using this information.

PROCEDURE

Tell the students to locate the settings in the book, and to illustrate the settings by drawing them on sheets of paper. They may color or cut and paste pictures on the papers to illustrate the settings. These sheets of paper will be the pages of the book. Ask them to make a title page that includes a pocket in which characters in the story may be stored. The pocket can be made by gluing an index card onto the paper and leaving the top part loose to store the characters. (A small sealable bag also may be used for the pocket.)

Next, tell the students to recall the different characters in the story, and to draw the characters on construction paper and color and cut them out. Punch a hole in each character and tie a 3-foot piece of yarn through the hole. Tie the other end of the yarn through a hole punched in the upper left-hand corner of the book. (The yarn needs to be long enough so the characters can be placed on each page of the book where they appear in the story.)

The books should be bound or stapled together. The characters should be placed in the pocket on the title page. As the students share the book, they move the characters to the different pages in the book.

SUMMARY

Responding to literature is a motivating way to help students develop comprehension, language, and communication skills. Students enjoy creating their own books. These books can then be placed in the portfolio along with the checklists used to assess the different skills.

ASSESSMENT

Have the students retell the story, then use a checklist to assess comprehension skills, language, and communication skills (see Appendix A).

ENRICHMENT

Have the students work in cooperative learning groups to role-play the book. Students may create a literature response journal where they describe favorite characters in the book and tell why they are favorites. The author may record the book on tape to be placed in the listening center.

A Good and Perfect Gift

Objective

The students will compose a well-structured paragraph following the guidelines discussed in class.

MATERIALS

- *Good and Perfect Gifts* by Barry Moser
- writing materials
- blank gift sheets of paper for each student

PREPARATION

Ask students to describe what a paragraph is. Review paragraphs, discussing the topic sentence and subtopic sentences. Clarify any misunderstandings. Construct blank gift sheets by dividing the paper into four equal parts (fold in half long way and fold in half again short way). Number the squares one, two, three, and four. Draw a circle in the center of the paper. Draw a bow on the top of the page. The paper should look like a gift box with four equal compartments and a bow on top.

PROCEDURE

Read *Good and Perfect Gifts* to the class and ask students to make predictions at various points in the story. Discuss the story, then give each student a blank gift sheet and proceed as follows: (1) Tell the students to write the best gift they received in the circle of the gift sheet. (2) Tell the students to describe when they received that gift in square one on the gift sheet. (3) Tell the students to write words that describe the gift in square two. (4) Write why the gift was special in square three. (5) Tell the students to explain if their gift is similar to or different from the character's gift from the story in square four.

With the boxes complete, have the students write one sentence from each area, beginning with the circle, moving to square one, two, three, and four. When the students have completed this task, they will have a well-written paragraph with a topic sentence and supporting subtopic sentences. Explain that the information from the circle is the topic of the paragraph. Therefore, it is the topic sentence. Also explain that the information from the squares forms the supporting sentences. Ask students to read their paragraphs and identify the topic and subtopic sentences working together in pairs.

SUMMARY

This activity is a fun way to help children compose a cohesive paragraph with a topic sentence and supporting details.

ASSESSMENT

Assess the students' paragraphs by checking to see that they followed the directions given to compose a well-structured paragraph. Check to see that they followed the paragraph form (topic sentence, supporting details, conclusions, etc.) discussed. Check for grammatical errors.

ENRICHMENT

Ask the students to write a story about a gift they plan to give to someone special.

Media Maze

Objective

The students will recognize and pronounce commonly accepted language by listening to correct pronunciation of the words.

MATERIALS

- newspapers
- magazines
- television, radio, and other media communications

PREPARATION

Tell students to keep a diary of unknown or unfamiliar words that they hear on television or radio or that they find in newspapers, magazines, or books.

PROCEDURE

Ask the students to compile their lists to find the most common or frequent words. Working on 10 words at a time, the students study their spelling, definition, and pronunciation. Special recognition is given when these words appear in speech or writing as an incentive for the students to place these words in their vocabulary.

SUMMARY

This is an excellent exercise for culturally disadvantaged or English as a second language students to acquaint them with commonly used language. The activity also is valuable in correcting pronunciation problems due to colloquialisms or slang.

ASSESSMENT

Ask the students to write a paragraph using the 10 vocabulary words correctly in the paragraph. Check the paragraph for correct paragraph form and grammatical errors. Check the vocabulary words used in the paragraph to see that they are used correctly and have the correct meaning implied or stated in the paragraph.

ENRICHMENT

This activity is a good way to integrate different subject areas. Many of the words the students choose will have specific meanings in particular content areas.

Sample Rubrics and Checklists

RECALLING DETAILS IN STORY RUBRIC (TO CHECK COMPREHENSION)

1. The student describes the plot. 20 points
2. The student describes the conflict in the story. 20 points
3. The student describes the characters in the story. 20 points
4. The student describes the setting. 20 points
5. The student understands the language that the author uses to develop the story. 20 points

DESCRIPTIVE PARAGRAPH RUBRIC

1. The paragraph has a topic sentence. 20 points
2. The paragraph has details relating to the topic sentence. 20 points
3. The paragraph is written in the correct format. 20 points
4. The paragraph uses descriptive adjectives and adverbs. 20 points
5. The paragraph contains five to seven sentences. 20 points

CREATIVE WRITING RUBRIC

1. Original, unusual ideas and details. 20 points
2. Organization - Includes title, beginning, middle, and ending. 20 points
3. Chooses words to convey meaning clearly. 20 points
4. Interest to audience. 20 points
5. Fluent, connected sentences. 20 points

WRITING RUBRIC

1. Heading, title, capitalized and punctuated correctly, details, no fragments or run-ons, neat introduction. 4 (excellent)
2. Heading, title, punctuation and capitalization, few details, main idea. 3 (good)
3. Heading, title, no main idea, no capitalization and punctuation, no details. 2 (below average)
4. No effort. 1 (poor)

WRITING CHECKLIST

1. Sticks to topic.
2. Uses capitalization and punctuation correctly.
3. Avoids fragments.
4. Answers the five Ws (who, where, when, why, what).
5. Uses descriptive words.
6. Follows writing conventions.
7. Cohesive transitions.
8. Uses prepositional phrases.
9. Avoids *and* or *but* at beginning of sentences.
10. Avoids repetition.
11. Uses a variety of sentences.
12. Has introduction and conclusion.

GROUP PARTICIPATION CHECKLIST

1. Accepts responsibility for tasks.
2. Works cooperatively with others.
3. Does his or her share in group work.
4. Contributes ideas to the project.
5. Completes tasks assigned.

SOCIAL SKILLS CHECKLIST

1. Gets along well with others.
2. Takes turns.
3. Is respectful of others' rights.
4. Has positive attitude.
5. Works cooperatively with others.
6. Shares materials with others.
7. Attentive to directions.
8. Listens to others' ideas.
9. Uses materials appropriately.
10. Uses language to solve problems.

LISTENING SKILLS CHECKLIST

1. Is able to sit still and pay attention to the speaker.
2. Listens attentively to speaker.
3. Is interested in topic.
4. Comprehends message of speaker.
5. Is able to listen to follow directions.
6. Interacts with speaker by asking appropriate questions.
7. Relates new information to existing schema.

8. Adds personal examples.
9. Retains information.
10. Applies information to new situations.

CREATIVE STORIES RUBRIC

1. Uses original or unusual ideas in writing stories. 20 points
2. Fluency and cohesiveness of sentences. 20 points
3. Flexibility of elements in story. 20 points
4. Very detailed, elaborate descriptions of setting, characters, and plot. 20 points
5. Imaginative and unique endings. 20 points

WRITTEN STORIES CHECKLIST

1. Title
2. Beginning, middle, and ending
3. Complete sentences
4. Punctuation
5. Capitalization
6. Organization
7. Setting
8. Characters
9. Plot
10. Conflict

RESEARCH REPORT RUBRIC—ORAL AND WRITTEN

1. Ideas and development 10 points
2. Organization 10 points
3. Word choice 10 points
4. Fluency 10 points
5. Conventions of writing 10 points
6. Oral presentation 10 points
7. Voice and tone 10 points
8. Gestures 10 points
9. Interest to audience 10 points
10. Visuals 10 points

ORAL COMMUNICATION SKILLS CHECKLIST

1. Speaks clearly and distinctly.
2. Pauses when necessary.
3. Maintains eye contact with audience.
4. Doesn't use monotone voice.

5. Demonstrates enthusiasm.
6. Uses gestures to emphasize points.
7. Conveys message.
8. Listens attentively.
9. Takes turns speaking.
10. Uses body language to gain attention (posture, moving around, etc.).

CREATIVE AND CRITICAL THINKING CHECKLIST

1. Can think of divergent solutions to problems.
2. Has many different ideas in relation to problems.
3. Lacks conformity in their thinking.
4 Sees problems from different perspectives.
5. Thinks of original, creative ideas.
6. Uses unique, imaginative ideas in problem-solving situations.
7. Analyzes problems to understand them more thoroughly.
8. Applies information in new and unusual ways.
9. Is able to synthesize information.
10. Is able to evaluate different ideas based on certain criteria.

IRA/NCTE Standards for the English Language Arts

The vision guiding these standards is that all students must have the opportunities and resources to develop the language skills they need to pursue life's goals and to participate fully as informed, productive members of society. These standards assume that literacy growth begins before children enter school as they experience and experiment with literacy activities—reading and writing, and associating spoken words with their graphic representations. Recognizing this fact, these standards encourage the development of curriculum and instruction that make productive use of the emerging literacy abilities that children bring to school. Furthermore, the standards provide ample room for the innovation and creativity essential to teaching and learning. They are not prescriptions for particular curriculum or instruction.

Although we present these standards as a list, we want to emphasize that they are not distinct and separable; they are, in fact, interrelated and should be considered as a whole.

1. Students read a wide range of print and nonprint texts to build an understanding of texts, of themselves, and of the cultures of the United States and the world; to acquire information; to respond to the needs and demands of society and the workplace; and for personal fulfillment. Among these texts are fiction and nonfiction, classic and contemporary works.

2. Students read a wide range of literature from many periods in many genres to build an understanding of the many dimensions (e.g., philosophical, ethical, aesthetic) of human experience.

3. Students apply a wide range of strategies to comprehend, interpret, evaluate, and appreciate texts. They draw on their prior experience, their interactions with other readers

and writers, their knowledge of word meaning and of other texts, their word identification strategies, and their understanding of textual features (e.g., sound-letter correspondence, sentence structure, context, graphics).

4. Students adjust their use of spoken, written, and visual language (e.g., conventions, style, vocabulary) to communicate effectively with a variety of audiences and for different purposes.

5. Students employ a wide range of strategies as they write and use different writing process elements appropriately to communicate with different audiences for a variety of purposes.

6. Students apply knowledge of language structure, language conventions (e.g., spelling and punctuation), media techniques, figurative language, and genre to create, critique, and discuss print and nonprint texts.

7. Students conduct research on issues and interests by generating ideas and questions, and by posing problems. They gather, evaluate, and synthesize data from a variety of sources (e.g., print and nonprint texts, artifacts, people) to communicate their discoveries in ways that suit their purpose and audience.

8. Students use a variety of technological and informational resources (e.g., libraries, databases, computer networks, video) to gather and synthesize information and to create and communicate knowledge.

9. Students develop an understanding of and respect for diversity in language use, patterns, and dialects across cultures, ethnic groups, geographic regions, and social roles.

10. Students whose first language is not English make use of their first language to develop competency in the English language arts and to develop understanding of content across the curriculum.

11. Students participate as knowledgeable, reflective, creative, and critical members of a variety of literacy communities.

12. Students use spoken, written, and visual language to accomplish their own purposes (e.g., for learning, enjoyment, persuasion, and the exchange of information).

Web Sites for Teachers and Students

FOR TEACHERS

Reading Online
http://www.readingonline.org

Reading Online is a peer-reviewed electronic journal published by the International Reading Association. The journal features articles, commentaries, columns, and reviews related to literacy instruction in grades K–12. The site also offers online communities for visitors to voice their opinions or post questions. A special mission of the journal is to support professionals as they integrate technology in the classroom, preparing students for a future in which literacy's meaning will continue to evolve and expand. To accomplish this, *ROL* invites readers to shape the journal's contents through participation and interaction.

Barnes & Noble.com
http://www.bn.com

This site is an excellent source for the educational supplies needed by teachers on a daily basis. Teachers will find a wide variety of books, magazines, computer software, reference material, and more on this user-friendly Web site. Barnes & Noble.com also offers free online courses.

Discovery School's Kathy Schrock's Guide for Educators
http://school.discovery.com/schrockguide

This site is designed to give educators more tools for teaching and learning. It includes teacher helpers, subject access, and search guides that provide links to new and useful Web sites.

Classroom Connect

http://www.classroom.com/home.asp

Classroom Connect is a site for K–12 teachers that focuses on Web-based curriculum and products. It is primarily broken down into two sections: classroom curriculum and professional development. The site includes links to lesson plans, an online store, and a university that offers instructor-led courses.

Beginning Teacher's Tool Box

http://www.inspiringteachers.com

This site is used as a support system for new student teachers and substitute teachers. Educators can take advantage of articles, professional and classroom resources, mentoring service information, and much more. This site also offers a free classroom toolkit and free teacher Web pages.

Teachers Helping Teachers

http://www.pacificnet.net/~mandel

This site allows teachers to interact with other teachers about the most effective lesson plans, the best educational links, classroom management, and even humorous tips on reducing stress. Book reviews done by other teachers are also available.

Teachers.Net

http://www.teachers.net

Teachers.Net has a little of everything. Teachers will find free lesson plans, a reference desk, newsletters, and even live chats and a job chatboard. The site also offers a mail ring of more than 8,000 teachers from around the world.

U.S. Department of Education

http://www.ed.gov/pubs

This site can be used as a tool to locate information on the latest policies and legislation issued by the U.S. government. Educators will also find newsletters, journals, and an online store where Department of Education publications can be purchased.

FOR STUDENTS

700+ Great Sites
http://www.ala.org/parentspage/greatsites/amazing.html
A colorful and fun-looking Web site especially designed for children of all ages. Students will find links to hundreds of exciting sites about history, music, astronomy, sports, and much more.

Yahooligans
http://www.yahooligans.com
Yahooligans is a Web guide made for children. It includes sections on arts and entertainment, science and nature, news around the world, and many other educational topics that children will find fun and exciting.

Stately Knowledge
http://www.ipl.org/youth/stateknow
This site offers facts about every state in the United States. It can make a great homework helper for students with history questions. They can also use one of the knowledge charts to compare state size and population, or use one of the links provided to get even more information.

Weather.Com: The Weather Channel
http://www.weather.com
Weather.Com is a site that offers visitors all kinds of important weather information and updates. Breaking weather and local ski conditions, U.S. and world weather forecasts, and even financial forecasts are just a few of the many topics available on this site.

White House for Kids
http://www.whitehouse.gov/WH/kids/html/home.html
This site is meant to make children more familiar with the White House and how it is run on a daily basis. It supplies facts about previous presidents and includes details on important moments in U.S. history.

Publishers of Student Work

Chart Your Course!
P.O. Box 6448
Mobile, AL 36660

Child Life
1100 Waterway Boulevard
Box 567
Indianapolis, IN 46206

Children's Album
1320 Galaxy Way
Concord, CA 94520

Cricket
315 5th Street
Box 300
Peru, IL 61354

Daybreak Star: The Herb of Understanding
United Indians of All Tribes Foundation
P.O. Box 99100
Seattle, WA 98199

Highlights for Children
803 Church Street
Honesdale, PA 18431

Jack and Jill
1100 Waterway Boulevard
Box 567
Indianapolis, IN 46206

Merlyn's Pen: The National Magazine of Student Writing
Box 1058
East Greenwich, RI 02818

Quarterly Magazine
Children's Express
30 Cooper Square
New Your, NY 10003

Shoe Tree
National Association of Young Writers
P.O. Box 452
Belvedere, NJ 07832

Writing!
c/o Student Writing Department
60 Revere Drive
Northbrook, IL 60062-1563